EVERYTHING

YOU NEED TO KNOW ABOUT...

Playing the
Guitar

EVERYTHING

YOU NEED TO KNOW ABOUT...

Playing the Guitar

JACK WILKINS AND PETER RUBIE

David & Charles

A DAVID & CHARLES BOOK
David & Charles is a subsidiary of F+W (UK) Ltd.,
an F+W Publications Inc. company

First published in the UK in 2004
First published in the USA as The Everything® Guitar Book,
by Adams Media Corporation in 2002

Project Manager Ian Kearey
Cover Design Ali Myer

A catalogue record for this book is available from the British Library.

ISBN 0 7153 2056 4

Printed in Great Britain by CPI Bath
for David & Charles
Brunel House   Newton Abbot   Devon

Visit our website at www.davidandcharles.co.uk

David & Charles books are available from all good bookshops;
alternatively you can contact our Orderline on (0)1626 334555 or
write to us at FREEPOST EX2110, David & Charles Direct,
Newton Abbot, TQ12 4ZZ (no stamp required UK mainland).

Contents

Introduction

Although the guitar has been around since the Stone Age, we think of it more as a 20th-century instrument – from the turn-of-the-century concert hall performances of Segovia, to the rural blues mythology of Robert Johnson (who played so movingly it was said he had sold his soul to the Devil for the gift), to the startling electric jazz guitar of Charlie Christian, and on to the arrival of brilliant and outlandish rock guitarists, such as Jimi Hendrix, in the 1960s.

The guitar itself is a remarkable instrument. The six strings of the guitar have a musical range of more than three octaves, more than half that achieved by a piano, and the strings can be sounded together, giving the guitar the sense of being a small orchestra. It is more intimate and in some ways more responsive to a player's mood than almost any other instrument, and has both a pure singing soprano as well as a resonant bass – not bad for a musical instrument 1m (3ft) long that weighs less than most house cats.

The guitar has many forebears and cousins across the world – the lute, the Middle-Eastern *oud*, the Indian *sitar*, the banjo, the *koto* of Japan, the *bouzouki* of Greece, the *vihuela*, the *yue-chin, chirar, balalaika, rehab, kayakeum, santir, ombi, vambi, nanga, samisen* ... and on and on.

Guitar players number more self-taught musicians among their ranks than those of almost any other instrument. That's because it is easy to play simply, and very difficult to play well. Unlike other instrumentalists, guitarists are infamous for not being able to read music well. In fact, a joke among musicians goes: how do you get guitar players to stop playing? The answer: put a sheet of music in front of them and make them read it.

This book introduces you to an amazing instrument that has more personalities and ways to make music than possibly any other, and gives you some ideas and suggestions about that variety. There are ideas on what to practise, how to practise, and a few of the great guitarists of all styles and musical genres that you should listen to.

But most of all, you should practise a little every day, even if it's for only ten minutes, and don't worry if it doesn't sound good or you think it's all wrong. The key is consistency. Despite the sore fingertips, keep at it; it will all come right eventually.

If you can play a musical instrument, the personal rewards are wonderful. If you're lucky, your guitar and your music will take you around the world and into the homes and cafés and hearts of people with whom you may have little else in common except the language of music. And that is truly something worth striving for.

CHAPTER 1

History
of the Guitar

In the Beginning...

The guitar, or something a lot like it, has been around since the dawn of time. One day, a Stone Age hunter stuck the end of his bow into his mouth and started twanging the bowstring. And so the guitar was born. This is not just a wild guess. The first picture we have of the 'guitar' is in Trois Frères, in the south of France. In a Paleolithic cave painting, a figure is seen wearing a mask with a bow fastened to it. He holds the instrument in his left hand and plucks it with his right. A similar instrument, called the *okongo* or *cora*, is still used in parts of Africa to this day.

Early Forms of the Guitar

In the pre-Christian Babylonian, Egyptian and Hittite cultures of the Middle East, and on through Roman Italy, Greece and Turkey in the Near East, varying types of stringed instruments developed with certain aspects in common. Each had some sort of soundbox, long necks and cords or strings that were stretched over the soundbox and along the neck and fastened at one end. As players used one hand to strum (perhaps with a plectrum of some sort) and the other to stop the strings at various points along the neck, they could sound a wide variety of notes, both singly and together. Around 1400 BCE, for example, there is evidence that the Hittites played a four-stringed guitar-like instrument that had a characteristic figure-eight rounded shape.

Apollo, the Greek god of archers, is also, by a strange quirk of fate, the god of music. His lyre was composed of a turtle shell, with strings made of sheep gut or fibre stretched across it.

The Evolution of the Modern Guitar

The Four-Course Guitar

The Romans brought their *tanbur* or *cithara* to Spain around 400. In the 8th century, the conquering Arab Moors introduced the *ud*. By the beginning of the 13th century, there are a number of references and pictures of guitar-like instruments throughout Europe. It is possible that makers of the Roman-style *cithara* and the Arabic *ud* influenced one another, so that by 1200 the four-string guitar had evolved into two types: the *guitarra morisca* (Moorish guitar), which had a pear-shaped, rounded back, a wide fingerboard and several soundholes, rather like a lute; and the *guitarra latina* (Latin guitar), which resembled a small version of the modern guitar, with one soundhole and a narrower neck. This early instrument was a 'four-course' guitar, and is the probable forerunner of the modern ukulele. (Each pair of strings was called a *course*.)

In 1487, Johannes Tinctoris described a Spanish instrument called the *vihuela*, whose sides 'curved inward on both sides', and another instrument invented by the people of Catalonia, 'which some call the *guiterra* and others the *ghiterne*'. He added that because 'of the thinness of its sound... it was being used much more often by women to accompany love songs, than by men'. In Italy, these instruments were known as the *viola da mano* and *chitarra*.

The Six-Course Guitar

While the *guiterra* was small and had four courses, the *chitarra* was larger and had six courses. Both had thongs or cords tied at various places along the neck to make frets or square-like divisions of the neck. They became the instrument of choice for wandering troubadours or minstrels, who were virtual one-man bands, having to master pipes, whistles, flutes, songs, storytelling and anything else that would earn them money and keep them from facing the displeasure of aggravated patrons.

Minstrels did not use 'guitars' to accompany their stories, but to play small instrumental interludes between verses or tales or to sing folk songs.

Here's how a Swiss poet named Amarcius described a minstrel's performance in the 11th century: 'When the citharist appears, after arranging for his fee, and proceeds to remove his instrument from its cover of oxhide, the people assemble from far and near, fix their eyes upon him and listen with soft murmurs as he strikes the strings with his fingers stretched far apart, strings which he himself has fashioned from sheep gut, and which he plays now tenderly, now with harsh booming sounds.'

The Lute

The lute held sway as the major plucked stringed instrument for a long while, but it had a number of drawbacks. First of all, there was no standard lute, so some were large and some smaller; some had eight strings, others 12 or even more; and they were an absolute devil both to play and to keep in tune.

Soon after the reign of Henry VIII, around the middle of the 16th century, the guitar began to become a more popular stringed instrument, but for some time to come, rival camps of lutenists and guitarists would lose no opportunity to badmouth the others' instrument and musicianship. In 1556 in France, for example, it was reported that while the pear-shaped lute had been a popular instrument, people were playing the guitar even more.

A keen musician himself (and rumoured to be the composer of 'Greensleeves'), Henry VIII had more than 20 guitars among his collection of musical instruments in Hampton Court Palace.

Compositions for the Guitar

The earliest known music for the guitar was written for the *vihuela*. 'El Maestro' by Luis Milan, a Spaniard, was published in 1535 for the use and enjoyment of Spanish courtiers and aristocracy. Seven books of music survive, written in tablature. This early form of music is a sort of diagram, showing each string of the guitar and indicating where it should be stopped along the neck. Above the diagrams are notes indicating time values, or how long each note should be sounded. The diagrams show pieces of varying degrees of difficulty, including a series of regal dances known as *pavanes*.

Ten years later, Alonso Mudarra published a music book called *Tres Libros de Musica en Cifras para Vihuela*. This book contains several sophisticated, sometimes even dissonant, pieces that include a recurrent bass line which gives the music a syncopated, energetic feel.

By the early 17th century, there were a number of books and tutors on playing the guitar, particularly in France, where the instrument had become popular. Adaptations of lute music and arrangements of dances and fantasias encouraged the use of the guitar as a member of an ensemble or as an accompaniment to songs.

Early guitars had gut strings in courses or pairs, with a variety of tunings. A four-course guitar had ten frets and was tuned to FCEA, GCEA or CFAD. The top three strings were tuned in unison, while the bass string (which could be F or G) was tuned in octaves, or eight notes apart.

The music of this period was not played in such a rigid structure as classical music is today. There was room for improvisation, particularly when it came to variations of melodic phrasing and ornamentation. Advanced players, as always, could perform florid single-note passages and counterpoint and figured bass runs. Generally, however, the fashion for most players of the guitar at this time was for rather basic playing, mainly strummed chord patterns.

By 1600, the five-course guitar had replaced the earlier four-course and six-course guitars. The tuning also became more standardized, predominantly ADGBE. The Italian guitarist Giovanni Paolo Foscarini wrote some sophisticated new pieces for the instrument in the 1630s, while his fellow countryman, Francesco Corbetta, became one of the foremost virtuosos on the guitar, travelling widely throughout Europe and popularizing the instrument.

Many Musical Modifications

At the end of the Baroque period, two significant changes occurred. The five courses were replaced by six single strings, and they were tuned in the modern style of EADGBE. At the end of the 18th century, Federico Moretti wrote the first standardized book on the six-string guitar, *The Principles of Playing the Guitar with Six Strings*.

Many changes were taking place musically by this time. The modern piano first appeared, and, as it did, the guitar began to fade from popularity and was considered a more frivolous instrument of seduction and amour. A German diarist wrote, 'The flat guitar with its strum we shall happily leave to the garlic-eating Spaniards.'

Romance, lasciviousness and the guitar have been fairly consistent partners for a while, not just in the modern age of heavy-metal rockers. For example, Ronsard, a famous French poet of the 15th century, wrote:

It is the ideal instrument
For ladies of great learning,
Lascivious ladies also play
To advertise their yearning.

Gaspar Sanz, guitarist to the viceroy of Aragon, Spain, was as much a philosopher as a musician. His comments about the instrument and its players stand as well today as they did when he wrote the introduction to his method book on the guitar in the late 17th century: '[The guitar's] faults... lie in whoever plays it, and not in the guitar itself, for I have seen some people accomplish things on one string for which others would need the range of an organ. Everyone must make of it what he can, good or bad.'

The Napoleonic wars, at the turn of the 19th century, were responsible for repopularizing the guitar. The wars, which were fought throughout Europe, reintroduced Europeans to the guitar-based music of Spain. This period led to the work of such composers and performers as Fernando Sor, Mauro Guilliani, Matteo Carcassi and Ferdinando Carulli.

The first modern concerto for guitar and orchestra, Concerto No. 1 in A major, was composed and performed by the Italian virtuoso Mauro

Guilliani. Among other things, it uses the right-hand thumb for bass notes, and it has a strong orchestral structure, with variations on a theme, a slow second movement and finally a lively third movement.

Classical Guitar

Two people are responsible for the classical guitar as we know it today. The first was the brilliant guitar maker Antonio Torres, who revolutionized the building of a guitar, making a careful study of how it made its sound, where it came from and how he could improve it. The second was the Spanish virtuoso Francisco Tarrega.

The Torres guitar, developed between the 1850s and the 1890s, had more volume than previous designs. It included a larger, deeper body and an aesthetically pleasing shape that is familiar today. Torres was the first maker to use 'fan' bracing underneath the top. He once built a guitar with a spruce top and papier-mâché back and sides to prove his theory that it was the top that produced most of the volume.

Tarrega adopted the newly designed instrument, and composed and arranged hundreds of pieces for it. Ironically, Tarrega did not perform in public much. He was, however, an influential teacher, with a close circle of students and friends who acted almost like disciples in the world outside Tarrega's home and studio.

Then, at the dawn of the 20th century, there arrived a young self-taught musician named Andrés Segovia. Before Segovia, people believed it was not possible for a solo guitarist to perform effectively to a large audience in a concert hall. Since Segovia, the world has become filled with guitarists in concert. In 1924, Segovia made his debuts in London and Paris. He performed, transcribed, taught and discovered a tremendous amount of music for the guitar. He also encouraged many contemporary composers to write for the instrument. He managed to reawaken interest in J. S. Bach, and arranged many Bach pieces for the guitar, which he performed and recorded.

Of Segovia's many gifts to the world, perhaps his most lasting was to make the guitar *the* popular instrument of the 20th century. He also standardized the way guitar fingering is notated on scores (by showing the string number written within a circle over a series of notes that could be played elsewhere on the instrument), and settled the debate among classical guitarists about nails versus fingertips (by popularizing the use of plucking the strings with the nails of the right hand). By touring and performing throughout the world, he brought respect and recognition to the instrument and left behind a vast body of work and many pupils who went on to become maestros in their own right.

Flamenco

There are many different styles of playing, and before the guitar gained legitimacy in concert halls, a similar evolution had taken place in the bars and cafés of 19th-century Spain. Flamenco has three aspects: singing, dancing and guitar playing. It grew from the melding of Spanish folk cultures and the Middle Eastern influence of seven centuries of Moorish and Arabic occupation, particularly in Andalucia, in the north of Spain, where a large population of gypsies lived.

The Heartbeat of Spain

It was the Andalucian gypsies who turned flamenco into the heartbeat of Spain, although its roots are probably in Roman-occupied Spain. The composers Kodály and Bartók discovered in their research into folk tunes that beautiful folk songs have a way of ending up as 'beggars' songs'. In the same way, the outcasts of Spain – the gypsies – adopted and preserved the musical traditions of the Moorish Arabs who had once ruled the land.

What remained, and became idiosyncratically gypsy, were the traditions of whip-cracking dance rhythms and the troubadour's ability to improvise, composing verses about anything and everything at the drop of a hat. In the underground jargon of 18th-century Andalucia, someone *flamenco* was a dazzler, a 'dude with attitude'. The music came to be popularized by performers considered by many to be the haughtiest and most flamboyant of the gypsies.

Spain is a dancing country, and the simplest 19th-century village dance orchestra might consist of a guitar and a tambourine, with dancers wielding castanets. In the 1850s and after, it was also a country at war with itself; but whether royalist or revolutionary, the tradition was never to shoot a man with a guitar – at least, not until he was given a chance to play, anyway.

Flamenco on the Move

The rhythmic and melodic early forms called *seguidilla* and *rasgueado* developed new and exciting forms in the *café cantantes*, bars with areas for performers. Gradually, guitar players developed short instrumental melodic interludes with variations, called *falsetas*.

What had for centuries been campfire entertainment suddenly found itself on a stage attracting the attention and applause of Europe's leading writers, poets, painters and musicians – including Chopin, Liszt, George Sand, Alexandre Dumas, Edouard Manet and Jules Verne – who discovered the joys and inexpensive excitement of Spain on their 'grand holidays'.

The flamenco guitar sounds different from the classical guitar because cypress wood is used for the back and sides, instead of rosewood. The use of the capo (a clamp that goes around the neck and shortens the string length) also affects the tone, giving the strings a more treble sound.

Ramon Montoya is considered to be the father of modern flamenco guitar. Before his death in 1949, he pioneered the recording of the style and developed its traditions and techniques. In doing so, he enriched the music's vocabulary and established himself as one of the first flamenco virtuosos of the 20th century.

His real contribution, however, was to be the first person to break free of the role of accompanist and become established as a solo instrumentalist. When he performed in concert in Paris in 1936, he met with great acclaim.

It has been said that as flamenco has moved from the cafés to the nightclubs, the players have become more circus-like in the manner in which they play the guitar – wearing gloves, putting the instrument behind their heads, anything to attract and hold an audience's attention. Nevertheless, the 20th century produced some stunning players, such as Sabicas, Carlos Montoya, Niño Ricardo, Paco de Lucia and Paco Peña.

The Electric Guitar

Early Development

The European troubadour traditions of folk music and the spiritual music of African slaves evolved into a guitar- and banjo-based music that in time became ragtime and then jazz. The guitar's role was problematic, though, because it never seemed loud enough to cut through all the other instruments of the group. That was one reason for the banjo's popularity – it might not have been as sophisticated a musical instrument as the guitar, but in an ensemble situation it held its own against blaring cornet, braying trombone, squawking clarinet and the thumping of a drummer and the crash of his cymbals.

The concept of using the guitar like a trumpet or saxophone to play melodic solos began with the brilliant blues and jazz guitarist Lonnie Johnson. If you listen to his recordings made with Louis Armstrong in the mid-1920s, you can hear the two young virtuosos create a musical art form – jazz – in their Hot Five and Hot Seven sessions. Johnson followed this up with a series of terrific jazz guitar duo recordings (the first to be made) with another early jazz guitar virtuoso, Eddie Lang.

The development of the guitar moved from Europe to the USA when the German manufacturer Christian Friedrich Martin established the Martin guitar manufacturing company in New York in 1833. The guitars he made were different from those of the Spanish; they were bigger and used steel strings instead of sheep gut.

In France in the late 1920s and early 1930s, the gypsy outsider Django Reinhardt took Lonnie Johnson's single-note concept – he was no doubt also influenced by Eddie Lang's classic early recordings with the violinist Joe Venuti – and developed it using a revolutionary new guitar, the Selmer Maccaferri. This design had an enlarged body, a D-shaped soundhole and special internal strutting that made the instrument far louder than conventional guitars. What's more, Django was a near-genius on the instrument and played it with a fiery, inventive style that is still breathtaking to listen to.

More Volume

The search for more volume led Lloyd Loar, an engineer at the Gibson guitar company, to play around with electrified guitars and amplifiers. In 1924, his experiments with magnetic coils led to the development of a basic pickup, which was, in effect, a giant magnet shaped like a horseshoe that acted as a microphone for each of the strings of the guitar. The signal was then fed through an amplifier with a volume control and a tone control. It was all very rudimentary stuff. Gibson didn't go for the idea, however, and Loar left and formed the Vivitone company, which produced commercial guitar pickups during the 1930s.

The First Commercial Electric Guitar

The real breakthrough came in 1931, when Paul Barth and George Beauchamp joined forces with Adolph Rickenbacker to form the Electro String Company. They then produced the first commercially available electric guitar, the A22 and A25 cast-aluminium lap-steel guitar, known as the 'Frying Pan' because of its shape.

Strictly speaking, the 'Frying Pan' wasn't really an electric version of a traditional guitar, rather that of a lap-steel or Hawaiian guitar. However, in 1932 they produced the Electro Spanish, which was an archtop, or F-hole, steel-string guitar fitted with a horseshoe magnet. Gibson finally caught on, and adapted their L-50 archtop model into the now famous ES-150 electric model, which first appeared in 1936.

The musician who was to make the electric guitar a household word, Charlie Christian, was not actually the first electric guitar player. That role fell to Eddie Durham, who played a resonator guitar in Bennie Moten's jazz group from 1929 and recorded the first electric guitar solo, 'Hittin' the Bottle', in 1935, with Jimmie Lunceford's band. He then made some historic recordings in New York City in 1937 and 1938 with the Kansas City Six, a spin-off group of musicians from Count Basie's Big Band that featured Lester Young on clarinet as well as saxophone. For the first time, the guitar was easily a match in volume and single-note improvisation for the saxophone and clarinet of Lester Young and the trumpet of Buck Clayton.

There was one fundamental problem with the electric guitar, though – it kept feeding back. The amplified sound from the speaker would cause the body of the guitar to vibrate until a howl started that could only be stopped by turning the volume off. Guitarists found they were continually adjusting their volume levels to stop their instruments from feeding back. The answer was to create an instrument that didn't vibrate in sympathy with its amplified sound.

The Solid-Bodied Guitar

There's no definitive agreement about who produced the first solid-bodied guitar. Guitarist Les Paul created a 'Log' guitar, using a Gibson neck on a flat piece of wood. He went to Gibson to get it into production, but Gibson, once again, were not impressed and turned him down.

At the same time, country guitarist Merle Travis was working with engineer Paul Bigsby, and they produced about a dozen solid-body guitar prototypes. However, the man who made the first commercially available solid-body guitar was Leo Fender, the owner of an electrical repair shop. In 1946 he founded the Fender Electrical Instrument Company to produce Hawaiian guitars and amplifiers. Encouraged by an employee, George Fullerton, they designed and eventually marketed a line of solid-body guitars called the Fender Broadcaster in 1950. The Gretsch drum company manufactured drums called Broadcaster, however, and told Fender he couldn't use that name. So Fender changed the name of his guitar to the Telecaster. The rest is history.

The solid-bodied electric guitar paved the way for the popularization of urban blues and an R&B boom in the 1950s, with such great musicians as Howlin' Wolf, Hubert Sumlin, Muddy Waters, B. B. King and so forth. These musicians in turn influenced a generation of young rock-and-roll players in the 1960s in England, including Eric Clapton, Jeff Beck, Robert Fripp and Jimmy Page.

And Beyond...

Perhaps the most revolutionary advance of the last 20 years has been the development of MIDI, or Musical Instrument Digital Interface, a computer protocol that allows computers, synthesizers and other equipment to talk to each other. While electronic music has been primarily a computer and keyboard-oriented process, the guitar synthesizer is coming into its own. In the past it has had some problems with delay and tracking (how quickly, in effect, you can play one note after the other), but that seems to be disappearing with each new generation of equipment.

An example of the new guitar is the SynthAxe, developed in Britain in 1984. This guitar synthesizer is played via an innovative fretboard touch system. The neck acts as a MIDI controller, allowing the player to produce a full range of synthesized and sampled sounds.

Other guitarists have experimented with adding extra strings to the existing six, ranging from seven to 42 or more. But one revealing factor seems constant: all the players of the experimental guitars end up continuing to use the traditional six-string guitar, regardless of whatever else they play.

Where we go from here is anyone's guess – but one thing is certain: somewhere in the background is likely to be the twang and strum of a simple six-string guitar.

History of the Guitar at a Glance

1700BCE Legend relates that Hermes, the Greek messenger of the gods, invents the seven-string lyre, the forerunner of the guitar. Meanwhile, at about the same time in Egypt, pictures of a guitar-like instrument are painted on the walls of tombs.

500BCE The *cithara* develops from the lyre.

1265 Juan Gil of Zamora mentions the early guitar in *Ars Musica*.

1283–1350 *Guitarra latina* and *Guitar moresca* are mentioned many times in the poems of the Archpriest of Hita.

1306 A 'gitarer' is played at the Feast of Westminster in England.

1381 Three Englishmen are sent to prison for making a disturbance with 'giternes'.

1404 *Der mynnen regein* by Eberhard Von Cersne makes reference to a 'quinterne'.

1487 Johannes Tinctoris described the *guitarra* as being invented by the Catalans.

1535 'El Maestro' by Luis Milan is published, and contains the earliest known *vihuela* music, including courtly dances known as *pavanes*.

1551–55 Nine books of tablature are published by Adrian Le Roy. These include the first pieces for five-course guitar. The addition of the fifth course is attributed to Vicente Espinel.

1674 The *Guitarre Royal*, by Francesco Corbetta, is published. Dedicated to Louis XIV of France, it further increases the guitar's popularity.

1770–1800 The five courses (doubled strings) are replaced by single strings, and a sixth string is added to the guitar.

1800–50 Fernando Sor, Mauro Guilliani, Matteo Carcassi and Dionisio Aguado all perform, teach, write and publish their compositions. The guitar begins to enjoy wide popularity.

1833 Christian Frederick Martin arrives in New York City and founds the Martin guitar manufacturing company.

1850–92 Guitar maker Antonio Torres develops the larger, more resonant instrument we know today.

1902 The Gibson Mandolin-Guitar Manufacturing Company is founded in Kalamazoo, Michigan, USA, and quickly becomes one of the most famous guitar manufacturers in the world.

1916 Segovia performs at Ateneo, the most important concert hall in Madrid. Previously, it was thought that the guitar did not have the volume for this type of venue.

1931 The Electro String Company is founded, and the A22 and A25 cast-aluminium lap-steel guitars, known as 'Frying Pans' because of their shape, are the first commercially produced electric guitars.

1950 The Fender Solid Body Telecaster first appears.

1960 The guitar is finally accepted as a serious musical instrument for study at the Royal College of Music in London.

1984 The SynthAxe makes its appearance.

CHAPTER 2

Famous Classical and Flamenco Guitarists

Andrés Segovia (1893–1987)

Andrés Segovia was a talented guitarist responsible for bringing the guitar into the concert hall. Without his efforts, the guitar would still be confined to campfires, small bars and other private settings.

Segovia was born in Linares, a small town in the southern part of Spain, a region famous for its classical-guitar and flamenco players. Guitar music was all around him from early childhood. According to one story, a local luthier (guitar maker) made little Andrés a small guitar, and that's how his studies began. Although Segovia was self-taught, he adopted many of the techniques and practices of Francisco Tarrega, the influential late-19th-century guitar maestro.

Segovia made his debut at the age of 16 in Grenada at the Centro Artistico, and his professional debut in Madrid in 1912. It was met with disbelief by many, because the guitar was widely believed to be incapable of proper classical expression, but Segovia stunned his critics with his skill. From 1916 on he toured South America, and in 1924 he debuted in London and Paris, becoming known as 'the ambassador of the guitar'. He made his American debut in New York City in 1928. He had a wide repertoire of lyrical works, which he played with great emotional expressiveness using his fingernails on gut strings; and he demanded silence and concentration from his audiences during his performances.

The Messenger

As Segovia grew older, he came to consider himself the messenger who would bring the guitar to the world concert stage so that it could take its place beside the violin and the piano. Before long, composers like Heitor Villa-Lobos began to write music specifically for the guitar. Segovia himself arranged many pieces from the classical canon for the guitar – most notably by J. S. Bach, whose works experienced a revival, and who posthumously enjoyed the popularity of a 20th-century composer. Segovia also wrote music for the lute and the harpsichord.

The central problem that Segovia faced during his early career was making sure the guitar's sound would fill a concert hall. Over the years, Segovia solved the dilemma through modification of his instrument: he worked to improve the guitar's natural amplification by using different types of wood and playing with its design. Modern technology lent a helping hand as well. During the 1940s, Segovia adopted newly developed nylon guitar strings, which improved the guitar's range and consistency of tone (and were more durable, as well).

Segovia's achievements did not end there. In addition to settling the long-standing nails-versus-fingertips debate by popularizing the use of plucking the strings with the nails of the right hand, he also developed a standard score notation for guitars, which showed the string number written within a circle over a series of notes that could be played elsewhere on the neck of the instrument.

Segovia played a Ramirez classical guitar from 1912 until the 1930s, when he met the German luthier Hermann Hauser. The maker was so impressed with Segovia's guitar that he changed the way he built guitars, and presented Segovia with a new instrument in 1937, which the maestro used until the 1960s.

Segovia's Gift

It can't be overemphasized that Segovia's most lasting achievement was to make the guitar *the* popular instrument of the 20th century. In addition to recording and performing, Segovia spent much of his life and career successfully influencing the authorities at conservatories, academies and universities to include the guitar in their instruction programmes with the same emphasis as that given to the violin, cello and piano. He continued to give concerts well past the age of 80. His early struggles are recounted in his 1983 memoir, *Andrés Segovia: An Autobiography of the Years 1893–1920*.

Julian Bream (1933–)

Julian Bream, born in London, followed in the steps of Andrés Segovia as a maestro classical guitarist and lute player, even though Bream played a steel-string guitar, which is not normally used for classical guitar music. In his work, Bream drew his inspiration from the Belgian gypsy/jazz musician Django Reinhardt.

When Bream heard a recording of Segovia playing 'Recuerdos de la Alhambra', he was captivated, and henceforth devoted his time to studying the classical guitar.

Sharon Isbin was the first person to be appointed Professor of Guitar at the Julliard Music School in New York in 1989.

Bream was largely self-taught (although helped by the Philharmonic Society of Guitarists), and he attended the Royal College of Music, where he studied piano and composition, because the guitar was not considered a 'serious' instrument at that time.

His public debut was at the Cheltenham Art Gallery in 1946, and he began broadcasting for BBC Radio in the late 1940s. He also took up the lute and studied and played music that dated back to the 17th century. In 1960 he founded the Julian Bream Consort, an ensemble of original instrument virtuosi who were successful in reviving the music of the Elizabethan era.

By the 1950s, he had won fame for his technique and mastery of a wide range of musical styles. Like Segovia, he encouraged composers to write for the guitar, but unlike Segovia, Bream supported fresh, sometimes dissonant, modern material, which he nevertheless managed to perform with a striking tone and great emotionality.

Christopher Parkening (1947–)

Parkening is one of the premier classical guitarists of the past few decades. In recognition of his achievements, he has been awarded an honorary doctorate in music from Montana State University, USA, where he teaches summer classes, and has received three Grammy nominations for best classical performance. Parkening performs more than 80 concerts a year; he is a skillful guitarist, and his music is full of beauty and inspiration.

John Williams (1941–)

Born in Australia, Williams began learning the guitar at the age of four at the knee of his father, Len, who was also a gifted guitarist. When the family moved to London in 1952, Williams met and studied with Segovia, and upon his recommendation entered the Accademia Musicale di Siena in Italy, where he won a scholarship and stayed until 1961.

In 1958, at the request of his fellow students, he was the first student of any instrument to give a complete solo recital at the Accademia Musicale. He began recording and touring, and in 1960 he was made Professor of Guitar at the Royal College of Music in London.

Williams was dubbed by Segovia 'the prince of the guitar', and his brilliant technique soon attracted worldwide attention. He and Julian Bream played and recorded a series of duets and recorded works as diverse as transcriptions of Scarlatti and Andre Previn's Guitar Concerto.

The older Bream encouraged contemporary composers to write for the instrument, but he was also instrumental in a revitalization of early music. Williams, on the other hand, has been in the forefront of breaking down the barriers between classical and popular music.

Williams has performed with flamenco guitarists, and at Ronnie Scott's Jazz Club in London, as well as in rock concerts playing steel-strung acoustic and electric instruments. His album *Changes* (1971) features arrangements of songs by the Beatles and Joni Mitchell, as well as a rock version of J. S. Bach's Prelude from the Suite in E major. The piece 'Cavatina' actually hit the pop charts briefly. In 1979 he formed Sky, a group that fused classical, jazz and pop ideas.

Ida Presti and Alexandre Lagoya were the first well-known 20th-century classical guitar duo. Presti had the unusual technique of using the sides, rather than the tips, of her fingernails.

Narcisco Yepes (1927–97)

Yepes was a Spanish guitarist of agility, precision and execution. He was the first to commercially record Rodrigo's Concerto de Aranjuez in 1955. In the early 1960s he began to play a ten-string classical guitar, which had additional bass strings tuned to C, B♭, A♭ and G♭. These extra strings helped him arrange and play the piano compositions of composers such as Albéniz and Falla on the guitar, as well as fuller transcriptions of baroque music by composers such as Teleman and Scarlatti.

Concerto de Aranjuez (1939) is one of the most famous pieces of music written for guitar and orchestra. It was written by the blind Spanish composer Joaquin Rodrigo.

Ramón Montoya (1880–1949)

Born into a flamenco-playing gypsy family, Montoya was influenced by Rafael Marin, who had studied with the great classical guitar master Francisco Tarrega. Montoya's playing was sophisticated and built on traditions, while adding new ideas and enriching the flamenco vocabulary. Early in his career in the 1920s, he accompanied many of the major singers and dancers in the Café de La Marina in Madrid, and won renown as a virtuoso player.

His most important contribution to flamenco, however, was to break free from the role of accompanist and become a solo instrumentalist. He recorded many flamenco records, but his early recordings, such as 'Granadina', made in Paris in the 1930s, are among some of the most exciting and extraordinary.

Flamenco guitars have a different sound than classical guitars, due to lighter construction, cypress-wood bodies and lower string action.

Carlos Montoya (1903–93)

Like his uncle Ramón Montoya, Carlos also became a successful and influential flamenco guitarist.

Part of a gypsy family in Spain, his interest in music and the guitar began at an early age. He first learned how to play the guitar from his mother. Later, he took lessons from Pepe el Barbero, who was the neighbourhood barber.

Carlos started playing professionally at the age of 14, accompanying singers and dancers in the cafés in Madrid. Two of the dancers he most often played for were La Teresina and La Argentina.

In the 1920s, Carlos began touring Europe, Asia and North America. When World War II broke out in 1939, Carlos was on tour with a dancer in the United States. He decided to settle in New York City, eventually becoming a United States citizen. By the end of the war, Carlos had expanded his repertoire to include blues, jazz and folk music. He was the first flamenco guitarist to tour the world with symphonies and orchestras. He performed on television and recorded more than 40 albums, including *Suite Flamenco*, a concerto he performed with the St Louis Symphony Orchestra in 1966.

Carlos Montoya transformed flamenco from a dance accompaniment to a serious form of guitar music with a style all its own. With his own style, he adapted it to other genres of music, an achievement that brought him the recognition and renown of an international celebrity.

Sabicas (1912–90)

Sabicas' real name was Agustín Castellón Campos, and he was born of a gypsy family in the north of Spain. A prodigy whose virtuoso style helped define modern flamenco, he left Spain in 1937 for Mexico, where he formed a company with the flamenco dancer Carmen Amaya that toured the world, making recordings.

By the mid-1950s, Sabicas had moved to New York, where he concentrated on a solo career as a concert and recording artist. His dramatic style and breathtakingly accurate articulation and technique became a blueprint for succeeding generations of flamenco players. A powerful improviser, he once said he could never play the same thing twice.

Paco de Lucia (1947–)

One of the leading flamenco guitarists of the late 20th century, Paco de Lucia was born in Algeciras, in the south of Spain, into a family of talented flamenco players. He began playing at the age of seven. Not only did his father encourage him to spend hours practising, but his house was sometimes visited by Niño Ricardo, a major flamenco guitarist who had studied and played with Ramón Montoya. De Lucia later discovered the recordings of Sabicas, whose speed and clean execution had a profound influence on the development of his style.

At 14, de Lucia won first prize in a major flamenco competition. In 1962, he accompanied the singing of his brother Pepe, and the two won the top prizes at the Jerez Concurso, a prestigious music festival. The following year he joined Jose Greco's dance troupe and toured the United States, meeting Sabicas and others.

He was greatly inspired by a trip to Brazil, and began a series of innovative developments in flamenco guitar style, based on new rhythms derived from Brazilian music and jazz. In addition to leading his own sextet, de Lucia enjoyed a long and creative partnership with leading flamenco singer El Camarón de la Isla.

Increasingly influenced by jazz, by the end of the 1970s de Lucia was working with John McLaughlin and Larry Coryell, and in the 1980s he and McLaughlin went on to work with Al DiMeola.

In 1991, he memorized and recorded Rodrigo's famous Concerto de Aranjuez, which he played with a flamenco feel. The release of 1999's *Luzia* heralded de Lucia's return to traditional flamenco, though he continues to play in other music forms with other musicians.

CHAPTER 3

Famous
Blues Guitarists

Charley Patton (1887–1934)

Born in Mississippi, Patton was considered one of the early innovative and influential figures in blues, ragtime, country songs and spirituals. His 'Pony Blues', recorded in 1929, became a commercial success that made him a star in blues circles. He played with a loose style that bent bar lengths and timing, though his style was nevertheless earthy and rhythmic.

Charley Patton was one of the great blues showmen. He often played at jukes (small bars) and on street corners. One of his tricks, later adopted by blues and rock musicians such as T-Bone Walker and Jimi Hendrix, was to play the guitar behind his back.

With careful listening, you can hear him play instrumental responses to his sung phrases. He evoked sounds from the guitar in a crude percussive style, snapping strings and drumming on the instrument. He also tuned his guitar higher than normal to give it a bright, penetrating sound. By the time of his death, he had become a legendary figure in the Mississippi Delta and had influenced countless other blues musicians.

Big Bill Broonzy (1893–1958)

Born in Scott, Mississippi, to a sharecropping family, William Lee Conley Broonzy began to play music at an early age. By the time his family moved to Arkansas, he already played fiddle, and by the age of 14 he was fiddling for tips at picnics, dances and other local events.

After serving in the army for two years, Broonzy went to Chicago, where he began learning the blues guitar with Papa Charlie Jackson, and that's when his blues-guitar career took off. Big Bill Broonzy's style covered a wide variety of blues styles, from ragtime and city jazz to traditional blues and spirituals.

This talented musician is considered to be the godfather of the Chicago blues scene, in large part because of his efforts to influence the younger generation of bluesmen, but his fame spread far beyond Chicago.

In 1951 he toured Europe, helping to introduce blues to France and England and opening the door for other American blues artists.

In 1955, with help from writer Yannick Bruynoghe, he wrote his autobiography, *Big Bill's Blues*, one of the first autobiographies written by a bluesman, which provides a fascinating look on his life and music. Two years after the publication of his book, Broonzy was diagnosed with throat cancer. Despite his failing health and the pain from his illness, he continued to perform until his death.

Blind Lemon Jefferson (1897–1929)

Blind Lemon Jefferson's story is part history and part myth. Despite his renown as a blues musician, we only have a few facts about the life he led.

Jefferson was born in Couchman, a small town in Freestone County, Texas. He was either blind from birth or since early childhood; in photographs he appears wearing clear glasses, which indicates that he might not have been totally blind and could possibly perceive light.

Undeterred by his blindness, Blind Lemon Jefferson spent his life travelling around from town to town in Texas, the Mississippi Delta and perhaps other southern states, playing and singing the blues as a street musician. He also made quite a few recordings and issued 43 records. During the 1920s, Jefferson sold more than a million 'race records' to the emergent African-American market.

In Dallas, in an area known as Deep Ellum – Dallas's version of the famed Beale Street in Memphis, Tennessee – Jefferson met Leadbelly (whose biography appears next). They played together for a few years, until Leadbelly was arrested and convicted of assault and murder charges. While his erstwhile partner served his prison sentence, Jefferson began his travels around the South.

Blind Lemon Jefferson played a Stella guitar, developed from 12-string guitars (made up of six pairs of strings, with the two highest courses tuned in unison and the others an octave apart), which were common in Central and South America.

Despite his fame and success, Jefferson met his death at the early age of 32, apparently a poor man living and playing in Chicago. The circumstances of his death remain unknown. One conjecture is that he died of a heart attack during a snowstorm. Another version of the story claims that he froze to death.

Leadbelly (1885–1945)

Huddie William Ledbetter, otherwise known as Leadbelly (a nickname he earned in prison because of his physical toughness), was born on Jeter Plantation in Mooringsport, Louisiana. His family were sharecroppers who were eventually able to purchase land on the Texas–Louisiana border, which they farmed (and were fairly successful).

The Young Years

Huddie was the only son and had the full attention of his family. When he was still a child, his uncle gave him an accordion and taught him to play. Later he also gave him a guitar, and Huddie began playing at parties and clubs.

For Huddie, music would always go together with drinking, violence and womanizing. At the age of 15, he got a woman pregnant. When, a year later, he fathered another child, the people of his town began to grumble, and Huddie decided to move elsewhere, at least for a while.

The Life of an Itinerant Musician

Huddie spent the next 15 years of his life roaming around Texas and Louisiana as an itinerant musician; when things got tough, he supplemented his meagre income by working on farms as a labourer. Eventually, he ended up in Dallas, where he encountered the young Blind Lemon Jefferson. They played music together until Huddie's arrest, the first of many brushes with the law that would follow.

Huddie (now known as Leadbelly) managed to escape, and returned to his home town to hide out. Soon, however, he grew restless and decided to move to New Orleans, where he took on a new name, Walter Boyd.

The new name protected Huddie from the authorities, but not from his own quick temper. Less than a year later, he got into a brawl, during which one of his relatives, Will Stafford, was shot and killed. Leadbelly was tried for murder and was found guilty, although he would always proclaim his innocence.

Leadbelly apparently had an uncanny ability to survive under any circumstances. In prisons, prison farms and hard-labour camps, he managed to keep his spirit up through music, and he soon became a favourite among other inmates and the prison guards.

Although he was sentenced to 30 years in prison, Leadbelly was released after seven years. Later, he claimed that he received his pardon from Governor Pat Neff after he sang the governor a 'please pardon me' song. Unfortunately, Leadbelly could never hold on to freedom for very long. Another assault conviction soon landed him on a prison farm in Angola, Louisiana, where he served his harshest term. According to prison records, he was often flogged in punishment for minor offences.

The 'Discovery'

It was at Angola that Leadbelly was 'discovered' by John Lomax, a folklorist from New York who travelled through the South under a Library of Congress grant to record music. Lomax was looking for folk and blues musicians, and he soon realized that the best place to look for them was in the prison system of the South. In July 1933, he met Leadbelly, who impressed him with his vocal style, the variety of his repertoire and his physical appearance.

In times of the Great Depression, prisons could not support all their prisoners, and many were released under the 'double good time' measures. Leadbelly got his chance as well, and went to join John Lomax in New York, where he performed for primarily white audiences who were interested in blues and the folk music of the black South.

Lomax also negotiated several deals, such as a contract to publish a book entitled *Negro Folk Songs as Sung by Leadbelly*, which would include

Leadbelly's story, 'discovery', transcripts of his songs and relevant explanations. Another deal was a recording contract with the American Record Company. Unfortunately, neither deal proved to be financially lucrative. Eventually, the professional relationship between Lomax and Leadbelly soured, and they separated in 1935.

Survival Instinct

To make ends meet, Leadbelly and his wife survived on odd jobs and welfare. In early 1939 he was arrested yet again, for assaulting a black man with a knife, and he served an eight-month sentence (his last) at Riker's Island prison. In early 1940, at the age of 51, Leadbelly was released, and went back to New York, where he joined the folk circuit with such talented musicians as Woody Guthrie, Sonny Terry, Brownie McGhee, Pete Seeger and many others.

Like Blind Lemon Jefferson, Leadbelly played a Stella 12-string guitar, but unlike him, Huddie used all 12 strings. His booming bass sound was made by using very heavy strings tuned down two tones below standard.

Soon, however, he was on the road again, convinced that he would find fame and make his fortune as an actor in Hollywood. Although this dream was not to be, he was relatively successful playing music at the local clubs and doing some recordings for Capitol Records.

Finally, after he had returned to New York for a period of three years, Leadbelly went on a tour in France, where jazz and blues were just becoming popular. While there, he experienced some health problems and was later diagnosed with Lou Gehrig's disease (lateral sclerosis), and he died six months later. The following year, his trademark song, 'Goodnight Irene', became an American Number One hit for a group known as the Weavers.

Howlin' Wolf (1910–75)

Chester Arthur Burnett, later known as Howlin' Wolf, was born in White Station, a small railroad stop in the Mississippi hill country. As is the case with many musicians, Chester was exposed to music from a very young age: his uncle preached at the White Station Baptist Church, and young Chester sang in the church's choir.

Chester did not have an easy childhood. When his parents separated, his father moved away to do farm work in the Mississippi Delta region. Meanwhile, his mother travelled around as a street musician, singing gospel songs for small coins. Chester went to live with his uncle, the preacher, who was a stern and difficult man. Later, when he began playing the blues, his mother disowned him, claiming that he was playing the Devil's music.

Becoming a Wolf

When he was old enough, Chester ran away from his uncle's house and managed to reach his father and his new family, who lived on a plantation near Ruleville, Mississippi. It was there that 13-year-old Chester first heard the blues. At that time, the great bluesman Charley Patton lived on a nearby plantation, and when Chester's father bought his son his first guitar, he also managed to persuade Patton to give Chester guitar lessons.

Howlin' Wolf played electric guitar with his bare fingers – an oddity for a Chicago bluesman – and his eccentric, slashing style made him a favourite guitarist of Eric Clapton, Jimmy Page, Stevie Ray Vaughan and Jimi Hendrix.

Until the beginning of World War II, Chester spent his time working on his father's farm and playing the blues with musicians like Robert Johnson, Charley Patton, Son House and Willie Brown. In addition to playing the guitar, he played a blues harmonica, which he mounted on a rack in front of his guitar. According to one version of the story, it was because of his voice, which was huge and raw, that people began to call him Howlin' Wolf. Another tale attributes this nickname to his family, who called him Howlin' Wolf because he was a 'difficult child'.

Rise to Fame

Howlin' Wolf did not take the blues seriously until the age of 38, when he set off for West Memphis, Arkansas, to start his blues career. Once there, he began working for a radio station, WKEM, and put together a band that included guitarists Pat Hare, Matt 'Guitar' Murphy and Willie Johnson, and harmonica players James Cotton and Junior Parker.

Wolf was a tremendous performer. Towering above his audience at over 2m (6ft 6in) and over 140kg (300lb), with his deep voice, mournful howls, harmonica riffs and the ability to sing from the soul, he had the power to captivate – and, some say, scare – his audience. Wolf was famous for the wild antics he performed on the stage.

In 1951, Howlin' Wolf finally got a record deal, recording two songs: 'Moanin' at Midnight' and 'How Many More Years'. Released the following year, they both made it to the Top Ten on Billboard's R&B charts.

Howlin' Wolf influenced many of the guitar-based musical genres of the second half of the 20th century, from the rock and roll of the 1950s, through Captain Beefheart's avant-garde and the classical rock of the 1970s, to the grunge-rock guitar music of the 1990s.

In Chicago

In 1953, Wolf moved again – this time permanently – to Chicago. Now he was 43 years old, and a talented bluesman with tremendous stage presence. Unlike the other blues performers, he preferred playing in small clubs and venues. During his Chicago period, Wolf continued to make some of his most successful recordings.

In the late 1960s, Wolf's health began to suffer. He survived several heart attacks and a car accident that damaged his kidneys. However, Howlin' Wolf would not abandon the blues. He made other recordings, sometimes teaming up with musical celebrities. He also went on tour in Europe, recording the *London Howlin' Wolf Sessions* with rock stars like Eric Clapton and the Rolling Stones. His last album, *Back Door Wolf*, included the fiery 'Coon on the Moon', the autobiographical 'Moving', and 'Can't Stay Here', a tribute to Charley Patton.

The Last Performance

Wolf gave his last performance in November 1975, at the Chicago Amphitheater. This was a huge blues event, with musicians like Luther Allison, B. B. King and O. V. Wright. Wolf performed his old songs, repeating his usual repertoire of crazy stunts, which included crawling across the stage during the song 'Crawling King Snake'. The audience went wild. Most people did not know that Wolf had crawled off his deathbed to perform at this event, and that when he finally came offstage, a team of paramedics had to revive him. Wolf died two months later during an operation.

Robert Johnson (1911–38)

Robert Johnson was born in Hazlehurst, Mississippi, into a large and rather tumultuous family. He was the son of Noah Johnson and Julia Dodds. Noah had left town to flee from a personal vendetta against him. Later, Julia rejoined her husband, his mistress and all their children in Memphis, and – bizarrely enough – they all lived in the same house. However, Julia decided to move on again, and she took Robert to Robinsonville, a small town across the border in Mississippi, where she later remarried.

Johnson's first job was farming, and according to some accounts, one of his first interests was women. He got married early; his 16-year-old wife, Virginia, and their baby died in childbirth in the same year, when he was just 19 years old. The life of a sharecropper didn't seem like anything to look forward to, and Johnson turned his attention to music.

The Life of a Bluesman

In his early teens, Johnson's main instrument was the harmonica. He took up the guitar during the late 1920s, studied with Willie Brown and later met Charley Patton. Shortly after Virginia's death, Brown introduced Johnson to Son House, part-blues musician, part-preacher, whose music was so intense it made a lasting impression on Johnson. Son House's influence can be heard in Johnson's recordings of 1936 and 1937.

But Johnson was a consummate musician in his own right; his talent was so awe-inspiring that myths grew up around him. According to one, he had sold his soul to the Devil at a crossroads at midnight in return for worldly success.

Although Johnson never really did get to enjoy much worldly success, he was recognized for his skill and particular style in the blues circuit of the Mississippi Delta. He spent a lot of his time travelling up and down the river, playing in levee camps, for road gangs and in juke joints, visiting family and friends in Robinsonville and Memphis. It seems that he could never spend more than a few months in one place. After a brief visit, he would always continue on his way, chasing gigs and women wherever he went. He apparently strayed as far as New York and Canada in later years, but he always came home to Helena, Arkansas, one of the most musically active towns in the Delta.

Robert Johnson often played a Gibson L-1 with a pin bridge and a round (as opposed to F-shaped) soundhole. Gibson built its reputation on archtops — or F-holes — but began to introduce flat-tops after 1926.

Johnson found it easy to attach himself to women who would take care of him. If he was going to be in any one place for a while, he developed a technique of female selection that generally kept him well fed and cared for. He'd find a plain woman, get on her best side with a few kind words, and he then knew that he could count on her affection and a place to stay.

A Talented Guitarist

Johnson was protective about his guitar playing and was acutely aware of other musicians ripping off his stuff. If someone was eyeing him too closely, he would get up in the middle of a song, make a feeble excuse and disappear for months. It all seemed a bizarre act of superstition, but there is a theory that Johnson may have been trying to hide his own method of tuning his guitar.

Other rumours told of Johnson's ability to play any piece of music he ever heard. He could be deep in conversation with a group of people and hear something – and he would never even stop talking – and later be able to play it and sing it perfectly.

Johnson's repertoire was not limited to blues, however. He often played requests for his audience, which sometimes included pop tunes, polkas, square dances, hillbilly tunes, sentimental songs, and ballads.

A Chance to Make Recordings

In the mid-1930s, Johnson met Ernie Oertle, who was the American Record Company salesman and informal talent scout for the mid-South. After an audition, Oertle decided to take Johnson to San Antonio, Texas, to record his music.

Johnson's first session in November 1936 yielded one of the songs for which he is most widely remembered: 'Terraplane Blues'. During his lifetime, none of his other songs would have the success of that tune. Meanwhile, Johnson's recording company, Vocalion Records, was growing disappointed in the low sales and did not extend any new offers to make recordings (by that time, he had released 11 records with them). His last record was released in February 1939, perhaps largely because his work was championed by John Hammond, a white promoter who had worked with Johnson on his second session.

Johnson's Last Job

Johnson played his last job at a juke house known as Three Forks, outside Greenwood (in the Delta region) that stood at the intersection of two highways. As usual, he had met a woman there. Unfortunately, this woman happened to be the wife of the juke-house owner. What happened next seems almost inevitable.

On 13 August 1938, Sonny Boy Williamson joined Johnson's Saturday-night performance. Both men sang and played the harmonica, and Robert Johnson played his guitar. According to later accounts, it was an amazing show, with lots of music, dancing, drinking and showing off.

As the night progressed, Johnson became more brazen, openly flirting with the juke-house owner's wife. Slowly, the good-natured party was growing tenser. During one of their breaks, someone offered Johnson an open half-pint of whisky. Although Williamson warned him not to drink from an open bottle, Johnson wouldn't listen. There was nothing Williamson could do.

Shortly afterwards, Johnson began to feel sick. He couldn't continue to sing, and was violently ill. Clearly, he had been poisoned. It seems that the jealous husband had laced the whisky with strychnine.

Johnson's Legacy

Although Johnson did survive the poison, his weakened system could not withstand pneumonia, which he had contracted a few days after the poisoning, while he was still recovering. At the time of his death, he was just 27 years old. It is uncertain where Johnson was buried. Most believe that his body lies in the graveyard of the Little Zion Church just north of Greenwood, Mississippi. However, there is another grave marked with his name, located at Payne Chapel in Quito, Mississippi.

The legacy of Robert Johnson's life has continued to live on. He influenced many musicians; rock bands such as Cream, Fleetwood Mac and the Red Hot Chili Peppers have covered at least one Robert Johnson song throughout their careers. In the mid-1980s, Johnson's life served as the inspiration for a Hollywood film, *Crossroads*.

Lonnie Johnson (1899–1970)

Almost uniquely among 20th-century musicians, Lonnie Johnson bestrides two of the most popular music forms of the early century – jazz and blues, defying categorization as belonging solely to neither.

Lonnie Johnson often recorded using a Stella 12-string, and a regular six-string Gibson archtop.

Johnson helped define the guitar's role in blues playing, and his melodic ideas and jaunty singing were on a par only with jazz's first recorded genius, the trumpeter Louis Armstrong. It's no coincidence that he recorded in 1927 with Louis Armstrong's Hot Five.

Armstrong may be considered the first jazz musician to step in front of a band and take an improvised solo, but Lonnie Johnson is the first guitarist to play a single-note improvised jazz chorus on the guitar. The two-guitar duets he recorded in 1928 and 1929 with jazz guitarist Eddie Lang – a musician who recorded several tracks for contractual reasons under the tongue-in-cheek name of Blind Willie Dunn – are groundbreaking in their inventiveness.

For more than 40 years, Johnson played blues, jazz and ballads, his versatility stemming in part from growing up in the musically diverse Crescent City, New Orleans. His first instrument was the violin, but he developed an unaccompanied style as a guitar player that was sophisticated, fluid and melodic. He signed up with Okeh Records, and between 1925 and 1932 he cut an estimated 130 tracks.

He moved to Chicago and returned to recording in 1939. In 1947 he recorded one of his biggest hits, the ballad 'Tomorrow Night', which topped the R&B charts for seven weeks in 1948. More hits followed, but by the late 1950s times had changed and he was earning a living as a hotel handyman in Philadelphia.

He was 'rediscovered' by banjo player Elmer Snowden, and enjoyed a major comeback, cutting a series of albums for Prestige's Bluesville subsidiary during the early 1960s. He also toured Europe with the American Folk Blues Festival.

Alas, in 1969, Johnson was hit by a car in Toronto, and died a year later from the effects of the accident.

Lonnie Johnson's influence was massive, from Robert Johnson, whose approach to guitar playing strongly resembled his older namesake, to Elvis Presley and Jerry Lee Lewis, each of whom at different times paid tribute with versions of 'Tomorrow Night'.

B. B. King (1925–)

B. B. King and his musical 'wife', his Gibson ES-125 guitar 'Lucille', is one of the most famous electric blues guitarists in the world. Inspired early on by Blind Lemon Jefferson and Lonnie Johnson, he also drew inspiration from early jazz guitarists, such as Charlie Christian. He developed a style of playing that used the guitar not just as a rhythmic accompaniment, but also as a sort of backup – or accompanying voice – when he sang, playing short, riff-like single-note melodic phrases. His first hit came in 1951 with '3 o'Clock Blues', and he went on to record many more, with big band accompaniment and jazzy phrasing.

The Gibson ES-125 is basically a cheaper version of Gibson's first electric guitar production model, the ES-150. During the 1940s, B. B. King used a Fender Bassman amplifier with his Gibson, and the combination became the standard for blues playing and recording well into the late 1980s.

CHAPTER 4

Famous
Jazz Guitarists

Django Reinhardt (1910–53)

Along with clarinettist Sidney Bechet, Django is considered one of the first major non-American figures in jazz. That he was a guitarist, then considered a lowly part of the rhythm section, is even more remarkable.

Born into a musical gypsy family in Belgium, he spent his childhood in a shantytown gypsy encampment outside of Paris. By the age of 12 he was playing banjo and violin at various gigs, and his first recordings, in 1928, were with an accordionist and someone playing a slide whistle.

That same year he had an accident with a candle in his caravan, and was momentarily trapped in a blazing inferno. He was so badly burned he was bedridden for 18 months, and his left hand was so injured that it did not seem likely that he would ever play a musical instrument again.

What Django did next was an indication of sheer genius and willpower. He came up with a completely radical way of playing the guitar using his two uninjured fingers on his left hand, barring the guitar neck occasionally with the fused stumps of the rest of his fingers, which gave his playing a harmonically distinctive, 'modern' sound. He also developed his right-hand technique, and his famous liquid chromatic runs were achieved by coordinating one shift of a left-hand finger with a down or up stroke of his plectrum in his right hand for each note of the phrase.

Django's first recordings on guitar were made in 1931 as an accompanist to a singer. Accustomed to listening to and playing the improvised forms of gypsy music, he was fascinated with American jazz and its parallels to flamenco. It's more than likely that he was listening to recordings of Duke Ellington, Louis Armstrong and guitarist Lonnie Johnson, and violinist Joe Venuti and his sides with guitarist Eddie Lang.

By 1935, Django had attracted the attention of visiting American musicians after he recorded with Coleman Hawkins and Michel Warlop's group. Record dates with Hawkins, Benny Carter, Dicky Wells, Eddie South and Bill Coleman resulted in some classic recordings. In 1934, the Quintet du Hot Club de France was formed, featuring Django on lead guitar, two rhythm guitars, a bass player and violinist Stephane Grappelli.

That Django and Grappelli work well on disc is clearly evident. That they distrusted each other for the whole of their playing career is not. Django was fiery, emotionally powerful and a naturally inventive improviser, but he was also impetuous and unpredictable. Grappelli was his opposite – cool, elegant, the 'boss' of the group who made it all happen behind the scenes.

At the outbreak of World War II in 1939, the group was in London. Grappelli stayed in England, while Django returned to Paris. Ironically, despite the fact that the Nazis despised jazz as 'degenerate music', after they occupied France in 1940, jazz seemed to flourish. Django reorganized the Hot Club de France, replacing one of the guitarists with a drummer, and Grappelli with a clarinet player.

Django had ambitions to compose for larger groups, but he was handicapped by the fact that he could neither read nor write music, and was dependent on others to take down his musical dictation.

After the war, Django went to America for a series of concerts. He expected to be fêted as a conquering hero, but the audiences were cool about his antics. He brought no guitar with him, for example, and his promoters had to rush around to find one for him to play. At his first concert, with Duke Ellington's band at Carnegie Hall, he was so late that Ellington was forced to offer an embarrassed apology for Django's non-appearance. Shortly afterwards, Django strolled on stage and began to play.

Adopting Electric

In 1946 Django was reunited with Grappelli, although he continued to play with other lineups as well. The major change in his career was his adoption of the electric guitar.

From 1937, he had played a Selmer Maccaferri, a specially designed guitar that was louder than the normal acoustic instrument. After his American adventure, he fitted a 'Charlie Christian' bar pickup on the Maccaferri, before eventually going all-electric in 1950.

The Selmer Maccaferri, made famous by Django Reinhardt, had a D-shaped soundhole, a flat cutaway and a two-octave fingerboard. The internal strutting was developed to enhance the volume and sustain. The guitars were launched in 1932, but by the end of the 1940s, Django was using a Stimer pickup, attached to his Maccaferri, through a small combination amp to get an electric sound.

By this time, Django's improvisation was being influenced by the newly emerging bebop style of Charlie Christian and Charlie Parker, with their more sophisticated and complex harmonies and rhythms. In the last couple of years of his life, Django went into semi-retirement in the village of Samois-sur-Seine, spending his time fishing, painting and playing billiards. Yet he continued to play with the emerging French bebop players, such as pianists Martial Solal and Raymond Fol, and alto saxophonist Hubert Fol. He recorded his last record on a purely electric instrument with this next generation of musicians.

In May 1953, he finished playing at the Club St Germain in Paris and caught the train to Avon, the station nearest to Samois. He went to a local bar for a drink and passed out. He was rushed to a hospital in Fontainebleu, but died at the age of 43.

Charlie Christian (1916–42)

Charles Christian was born into a musical family, in Bonham, Texas. His mother played piano as an accompaniment to silent films in cinemas, while his father sang and played trumpet and guitar. Christian's brothers, Clarence and Edward, also played professionally.

The family moved to Oklahoma City in 1918, and Christian's first instrument was the trumpet. This initial interest in the horn was an early indication of the musical breakthroughs he would make later in life, eventually producing horn-style improvisations on his guitar.

Novelist and family friend Ralph Ellison said that at the age of 12, Christian 'would amuse and amaze us at school with his first guitar – one that he made from a cigar box – playing his own riffs. But they were based on sophisticated chords and progressions that Blind Lemon Jefferson never knew.'

When Christian was young, he played in the family band and performed in Oklahoma City clubs. It was there that he first heard the tenor saxophonist Lester Young.

'Lester Young didn't bring Charlie Christian out of some dark nowhere', Ralph Ellison commented. '[Charlie] was already out in the light. He may only have been twelve or thirteen when he was making those cigar-box guitars in manual training class, but no other cigar boxes ever made such sounds. Then he heard Lester and that, I think, was all he needed.'

Christian was playing bass and guitar in the early 1930s in a band fronted by his brother Eddie, and was busy learning the solos of Django Reinhardt and Lonnie Johnson. He briefly led his own band, and later played bass and/or guitar with different bands in his area.

One of the first identifiable jazz guitarists was Brock Mumford, who can be seen in a picture of Buddy Bolden's New Orleans Jazz Band at the turn of the 20th century. Stonewall Matthews was an early 12-string player.

Christian had been experimenting with amplifying the guitar for several years in an effort to get a saxophone sound. Guitarist Mary Osborne recalled hearing what she thought was a tenor saxophone being played in a club in Bismark, North Dakota, in 1934, and discovering that it was Christian with a microphone attached to his guitar. But another seminal moment in Christian's life occurred in 1937, when he discovered the electric guitar.

Electric guitars with amplifiers were still new, although electric guitarist and trombone player Eddie Durham was already playing it as a solo instrument in Jimmie Lunceford's band. The new invention made the jazz guitar solo a practical reality for the first time. With the exception of Lonnie Johnson and Eddie Lang, jazz guitarists were part of the rhythm section, strumming chords. Now, guitarists could revel in the volume and sustain provided by an amplifier – in other words, they could sound like a saxophone or trumpet.

Christian and Goodman

Christian quickly realized the potential unleashed by the electric guitar, and he soon developed a 'saxophone style' of playing that was reminiscent of Lester Young.

He got himself a Gibson ES-150 (listed in 1936 at $77.50 or about £35, including a 5m cable), and by 1938 he was playing electric guitar in the Al Trent Sextet. By 1939, Charlie Christian's innovative guitar style was admired by many influential musicians in the jazz circuit.

Pianist Mary Lou Williams recommended him to record producer and jazz promoter John Hammond. In August 1939, Hammond set up an audition for Charlie with Benny Goodman, known at the time as 'The King of Swing', who also happened to be Hammond's brother-in-law. Goodman, who was white, was not only a great clarinet player, but was also a pioneer in touring with a mixed-race swing band.

The Gibson ES-150, launched in 1936, was based on the L-50 acoustic archtop, with the addition of a heavy, large bar magnet pickup and a tone and volume control. Christian later switched to the newer ES-250.

Goodman took some convincing. As Hammond recalled, when Christian arrived in Los Angeles, Goodman was presented with an apparent country bumpkin. Goodman gave Christian a cursory audition, asking him to busk on 'Tea for Two' without allowing him time to plug in his amp. He wasn't impressed.

Hammond said that he decided to convince Goodman by sneaking Christian onstage later that night during a concert at the Victor Hugo Club. Goodman angrily launched into 'Rose Room', a number he thought Christian wouldn't know. 'After the opening choruses Goodman pointed to Christian to take a solo', Hammond wrote, 'and the number, which ordinarily lasted three minutes, stretched out to forty-five! Everyone got up from tables and clustered around the bandstand, and there could be no doubt that perhaps the most spectacularly original soloist ever to play with Goodman had been launched.'

Goodman was won over. Christian's presence turbocharged the group, and Goodman made the most of the guitarist's new sound. His first studio recordings with the band were in New York City in October 1939, in a session that included 'Rose Room', 'Flying Home' and Christian's memorable solo on 'Stardust'. By 1940 Christian had recorded 'Gone with What Wind' and 'Air Mail Special', which featured snappy lines reminiscent of Django, and he had been voted 'Top Guitarist' by *Metronome* magazine readers.

While Goodman sometimes took credit for melodies actually composed by his sidemen, he nevertheless gave Christian partial credit for several classics, including 'Seven Come Eleven', 'Air Mail Special' and 'Solo Flight'.

Jam Sessions

The sextet made Christian a star in the jazz world, and helped legitimize and popularize the electric guitar as a jazz instrument. Some of Christian's last recordings were made in two after-hours joints in Harlem, in the cutting-edge hothouse environment of Minton's and of Monroe's Uptown House. Some music critics consider these the first recordings to show the 1930s swing style evolving into the fiery and far more harmonically and rhythmically complex bebop style.

Minton's, on West 118th Street, established by a retired sax player named Henry Minton, was located in a former dining room in the Hotel Cecil. The manager was a fellow saxophonist and former bandleader, Teddy Hill, who hired a rhythm section that included Thelonious Monk and Kenny Clarke. Jam sessions would sometimes last all night.

Christian was so into the jam sessions he bought a second amp to leave at Minton's. The band often included Kenny Kersey on piano, Kenny Clarke on drums, trumpeter Joe Guy and bassist Nick Fenton. Private recordings made by a jazz enthusiast at Minton's reveal Charlie Christian at his most inventive and experimental, as on the extended 'Swing to Bop'.

An Early Death

In summer 1941, Christian developed the first signs of tuberculosis. He was forced to leave the Goodman band's tour of the Midwest, and entered the Seaview Sanatorium on Staten Island. Count Basie's doctor kept an eye on him, while Teddy Hill came once a week bearing fried chicken and other goodies, and well-meaning friends sneaked him whisky and dope. He began to improve but found life dull, so one night in March 1942 he slipped out with some friends for off-limits carousing, caught a chill, and died. He was 25 years old.

Christian was buried in a small cemetery in Bonham. Although the exact location of his grave is not known, a marker and headstone were erected in his honour in 1994.

The amazing thing about Christian is that he recorded for a mere three years, but managed in that short time to influence many generations of musicians. He has been cited as an influence by blues and rock musicians as well as jazz guitarists. His style may lack some of the technical virtuosity of some modern guitarists, but Christian's lively, inventive single-note playing helped popularize the electric guitar as a solo instrument and ushered in the era of Charlie Parker and bebop.

Barney Kessel (1923–2004)

Born in Muskogee, Oklahoma, Kessel took on Christian's mantle from the mid-1940s through to the late 1980s. An innovative guitarist, he followed and developed Charlie Christian's swing style of playing, developing the harmonic possibilities of the instrument in a way that clearly showed a guitar player could do anything a piano player could do, and sometimes do it better.

Kessel got his first guitar at the age of 12 and was playing gigs with all-black bands two years later. At 16 he met and jammed with Charlie Christian, whose music he knew from recordings and radio broadcasts with Benny Goodman. A year later, he left for Los Angeles to try to make it as a musician.

Barney got a job in Chico Marx's band, and in the mid-1940s he was featured with Charlie Parker and Lester Young. He was also featured with Lionel Hampton in the Jazz at the Philharmonic concerts. By 1947 he had worked with a number of big bands, including Benny Goodman's and Artie Shaw's. That same year he went into the studio with Charlie Parker, and the results were classic bebop recordings that established Kessel as an accomplished and confident musician.

In 1952 he joined the Oscar Peterson Trio for a Jazz at the Philharmonic tour that visited 14 countries. He continued to record with Peterson and a score of other major jazz names. In the late 1950s and the 1960s, he became a major figure in the Los Angeles recording industry. His 1955 Trio album, *Cry Me a River*, featuring singer Julie London, is a classic of its type. He also recorded a series of records called *The Poll Winners* with bass player Ray Brown and drummer Shelley Mann. The records were so named because he and his partners consistently won jazz polls in *Down Beat*, *Esquire*, *Playboy*, *Metronome* and *Melody Maker* magazines.

Barney continued to play jazz and tour until 1992, when he suffered a stroke that left him unable to play. He continued to teach, however, and regained his ability to speak and move until he died in May 2004.

In 1934, Gibson introduced the large-bodied archtop Super 400, designed to give more volume.

Tal Farlow (1921–98)

While working in the seminal Red Norvo Trio with vibes player Norvo and bass player Charlie Mingus, Tal Farlow commented that there were only two tempos the group played: fast, and even faster.

Farlow is one of the two major influential bebop guitar players who led jazz into the 1950s after Charlie Christian, inspired by Charlie Parker. The other was his long-time friend Jimmy Raney, although Farlow is often considered the more influential of the two. Farlow's large hands helped him develop sophisticated chord voicings full of space and slight dissonances, while his inventive up-tempo single-note improvisations and imaginative use of artificial harmonics quickly won him a place as a major figure in jazz.

Both Barney Kessel and Tal Farlow used the Gibson ES-350, the first electric archtop with a cutaway, which was launched in 1946.

Born in North Carolina, Farlow began playing professionally at the relatively late age of 22. He was apprenticed as a sign painter at the insistence of his guitar-playing father, and intermittently throughout his playing career he returned to that trade. A reticent, self-effacing man with a laconic sense of humour, he once commented that playing a jazz solo was 'pretty much the same thing as painting a sign'.

Farlow was essentially a self-taught musician, inspired by hearing Charlie Christian on the radio with Benny Goodman. He moved to New York and quickly fell under the influence of major bebop musicians like Charlie Parker and Bud Powell, whom he listened to and occasionally played music with, in and around 52nd Street. He first came to prominence as a sideman with clarinettist Buddy DeFranco, but his breakthrough happened in 1949, when he joined the Red Norvo Trio at the recommendation of guitarist Mundell Lowe. The trio was one of the first expressions of modern chamber jazz.

In 1953, Farlow joined Artie Shaw's Gramercy Five and then led his own groups. He recorded several classic jazz records before marrying in 1958 and retiring from the limelight. He moved to Sea Bright, New Jersey, where he continued to play locally, teach guitar and, once again, work as a sign painter.

In the 1970s, Farlow came out of retirement, signed a contract with Concord Records and began to tour internationally again. In his declining years, he performed and recorded under the banner of the Great Guitars, with Herb Ellis, Charlie Byrd and Barney Kessel. A documentary, *Talmage Farlow*, was released by Lorenzo DeStefano. A compilation selected from Farlow's seven discs for Verve in the early 1950s, *Jazz Masters 41*, and *Tal*, also on Verve, are exemplary recordings of his work. Tal Farlow died of cancer in 1998.

Johnny Smith (1922–)

Before Smith ever picked up a guitar, he trained himself in classical music styles, which influenced his work. In addition, his large hands helped him to develop his own method of playing.

The uniqueness of Smith's technique is audible on all of his recordings, especially his most popular, *Moonlight in Vermont* (1952), which featured Stan Getz on saxophone. Many critics believe that this album solidified Smith's position as a jazz virtuoso. Smith is also known for his studio work at NBC. In the 1960s Smith retired from professional music and became a shop owner and teacher in Colorado.

The Gibson ES-175 was launched in 1949. It remains a mainstay for fusion and jazz players to this day, and has been used by Jim Hall, Joe Pass and Pat Metheny, to mention but three of thousands who have used the guitar.

Jimmy Raney (1927–95)

Jimmy Raney was the last word in jazz guitar. His sound was so cool, his solos so liquid, that the quiet, soothing music almost lulled to sleep the intensity within. Raney was influenced by Charlie Christian, but his style grew to encompass not just Charlie Parker but also the Lennie Tristano school of 'cool bop'. Indeed, Raney was sometimes called the Lee Konitz of the guitar, after the famous alto player associated with Lennie Tristano.

As a soloist, Raney emphasized lines inspired by those of Lester Young. He compensated for the emotional coolness of his improvisations by employing long melodic lines, cleanly articulated. One of the true innovators on his instrument, Raney exercised a profound influence upon guitarists of the 1950s.

Born in Louisville, Kentucky, Raney was influenced by his mother, who played guitar, and he studied with the guitarist Hayden Causey, whom he replaced in a band led by Jerry Wald. In 1944, Raney moved to Chicago, where he worked with pianist Lou Levy. In 1948 he joined Woody Herman's orchestra and recorded with Stan Getz.

After leaving Herman he played with Al Haig, Buddy DeFranco, Artie Shaw (1949–50) and Terry Gibbs, then joined Getz's quintet. It was this group that brought him to prominence, as he became known for his playing on several of Getz's important albums between 1951 and 1953. Raney replaced Tal Farlow in Red Norvo's Trio (1953–54) and worked at the Blue Angel, New York, (1955–60) in a trio led by the pianist Jimmy Lyon. He rejoined Getz in 1962, but remained with him only until the following year.

In the mid-1960s, Raney was active in New York as a studio musician on radio and television before returning to Louisville in 1968. He later played at clubs in New York (1972), gave a recital at Carnegie Hall with Al Haig (1974), and toured internationally with Haig and with his son Doug Raney, with whom he also recorded guitar duos. In the 1980s he performed and recorded as the leader of his own groups, which also included his son, although encroaching deafness hampered his ability to play in the last few years before his death in 1995.

Jim Hall (1930–)

Playing with a low-key cool and subtlety that are the jazz equivalent of a Japanese painting, Jim Hall continues to influence guitarists of many different styles and genres.

Like most guitarists of his generation, Hall was strongly influenced by Charlie Christian; he also found inspiration in the work of tenor saxophonist Lester Young. After attending the Cleveland Institute of Music, Hall moved to Los Angeles to study classical guitar with Vincent Gomez. In 1955, he helped to found the Chico Hamilton Quintet. He then joined the Jimmy Giuffre Three in 1956.

In 1961, Hall became a part of Sonny Rollins's quartet, where he recorded the guitar-tenor saxophone classic 'The Bridge', after duets with Lee Konitz and a tour with Ella Fitzgerald. In 1962 he helped lead a quartet with Art Farmer, while occasionally recording with Paul Desmond. He then moved to New York, where his career turned almost exclusively to studio work.

Since then he has, for the most part, been a band leader, working on a variety of his own projects for different record labels and recording two duet classics with pianist Bill Evans. In 1999 he collaborated with some younger musicians to release *Jim Hall and Pat Metheny*, which found the two guitar virtuosos from different eras pushing each other on songs and synthesizing into improvisations.

John L. 'Wes' Montgomery (1925–68)

Wes Montgomery is considered to be one of jazz's most innovative and inspirational guitarists. His influences included Charlie Christian and, later, the saxophonist John Coltrane, with whom he played briefly in an unrecorded group.

Although his guitar-playing was innovative and without compare, Montgomery did not experience any real commercial success until late in his career. Montgomery's signature achievement is, without a doubt, his expansive work using octaves.

Montgomery came from a musical family and taught himself guitar by learning the solos of Charlie Christian and Django Reinhardt, from whom he developed the idea of playing octaves. He tried to use a pick in the conventional style, but eventually opted to use his thumb, because he preferred the thick warm sound it produced. In the late 1940s Montgomery played with Lionel Hampton's big band. After his stint with Hampton, he went back to Indianapolis and lived a normal life – he had a non-musical job and played as many gigs as he could get.

During this slow period in his career, Montgomery compiled his first album, called *The Wes Montgomery Trio* (1959); the album featured his brother Buddy on pianos and vibraphone, and another brother, Monk, on the bass guitar.

Montgomery also received a lot of recognition for *The Incredible Jazz Guitar of Wes Montgomery* (1960). This album brought him to the forefront of jazz music, and it wasn't long after that he was invited to play with the John Coltrane Sextet.

To date, Montgomery's Riverside sessions (1959–63) are considered to be his most inventive jazz recordings. They featured some of the most prominent musicians of the era, including George Shearing, Tommy Flanagan, James Clay, Victor Feldman, Hank Jones, Johnny Griffin and Mel Rhyne. Montgomery's subsequent projects were a departure from straight jazz. He worked with Don Sebesky and Creed Taylor, and became interested in experimentation with orchestral performance.

His ingenuity paid off in a terms of popular acceptance. The records widened his appeal from a pure jazz base. Montgomery enjoyed branching out into other styles and genres; he spent the rest of his career, until his untimely death from a heart attack, experimenting with 'pop' sounds.

Today, Montgomery's legacy lives on – you can hear glimpses of his style in the music of Pat Metheny.

Pat Martino (1944 –)

Pat Martino is the stage name of Pat Azzara. Born in Philadelphia, he made an early appearance on the jazz scene – he had his first professional gig at the age of 15. Martino worked with many other jazz musicians, including Willis Jackson, Red Holloway and John Handy, who taught him avant-garde jazz, rock, pop and world music, and helped him develop his advanced hard bop style.

In 1976, Martino became ill and was diagnosed with a brain aneurysm. He underwent surgery, which was successful, but caused almost complete memory loss. According to some stories, he actually listened to his old recordings in order to try to remember how he had played and to help him relearn his craft. Martino worked hard and persevered. A decade later, he was on stage again, playing jazz guitar in a triumphant comeback, and he is still playing today.

Joe Pass (1929–94)

A hard-hitting bebop guitarist early on in his career, Pass became known as a great solo performer. His outstanding technique, recorded in the *Virtuoso* series of records on the Pablo label, gave him the deserved popular fame and renown that had eluded him in his earlier career.

Hailing from Philadelphia (and influenced by the troubled but virtuoso jazz guitarist Billy Bean), Pass began playing in a few swing bands and was with Charlie Barnet for a time in 1947. After military service, Pass became a drug addict, spending nearly a decade in and out of prison.

While he was recovering at the Synanon Halfway House, along with other musicians, the Santa Monica city council decided to disband the house. In order to make money to establish the halfway house outside the city limits, the talents of the recovering addicts were put to use. They borrowed instruments and went into a recording studio to record a series of original jazz tunes. *Sounds of Synanon* (1962) made such a stir that it brought Pass instant recognition as a new jazz talent. He followed this record with his first as a leader, *Catch Me*, and then the seminal *For Django*, before going on to record several other albums for the Pacific Jazz and World Pacific labels.

In 1974, Pass signed with Norman Granz's Pablo label and issued *Virtuoso*, the first of his solo guitar recordings. After that he recorded both unaccompanied and with small groups, including artists Neils Hennig, Osted Pedersen, Sarah Vaughan, Ella Fitzgerald, Duke Ellington, Oscar Peterson, Milt Jackson and Dizzy Gillespie, until his death from cancer.

Guitarist John McLaughlin popularized the fibreglass-and-round-backed Ovation, as well as the Gibson EDS-1275, a double-necked guitar made up of six-string and 12-string necks on the one large body.

George Benson (1943–)

Benson's musical career began in childhood; by the age of 17, he had his own rock band. Soon, however, he discovered that he preferred jazz. Like so many other guitarists, Benson's main jazz influences were Charlie Parker and Charlie Christian.

During the late 1960s and early 1970s, Benson perfected his jazz style and moved around between several record labels. News of his abilities spread throughout the jazz world. Benson was quickly crowned the next jazz maestro in a long line of well-known and well-respected musicians.

Despite all the acclaim of his peers, Benson turned away from guitar and jazz, and switched to pop music, focusing on his vocal talent. This change proved very profitable, as he was catapulted into stardom with his song 'This Masquerade' from the album *Breezin'* (1976). Subsequently, he teamed up with producer Quincy Jones and recorded *Give Me the Night* (1980), which turned out to be the best-selling album of his career. Benson's crossover attempt was a complete commercial success – but true-blue jazz fans weren't very pleased.

Today, Benson is best known for his vocal career, but that popular association has done nothing to diminish the power of his legacy as one of the world's greatest jazz guitarists. Benson's major jazz achievements remain performing with Brother Jack McDuff's band and recording with Miles Davis on *Miles in the Sky*.

Jack Wilkins (1944–)

Wilkins, born in Brooklyn, wanted to be a jazz artist from the moment he picked up a guitar when he was 13. Even then, he was aspiring to play like such great artists as Johnny Smith, Bill Evans and Freddie Hubbard. These inspirations have been motivating him to perfect his technique and go to new places with his approach to chords for the last several decades.

Windows (1973) was the first Wilkins album that showed him to be above the rest. The album received phenomenal reviews for being a breakthrough record in respect to its style. As Wilkins progressed, he recorded with many different artists, such as the Brecker Brothers and Kenny Drew, Jr.

Alan Holdsworth, the remarkable jazz-rock fusion player, plays a SynthAxe on his album *Atavachron* (1986). The SynthAxe is an innovative synthesizer guitar with a fretboard touch system. Guitarists who have extensively used guitar synthesizers include John Abercrombie and Pat Metheny.

Throughout his career, Wilkins has performed with a vast number of jazz musicians. He has participated in a number of international festivals, sharing the stage with Stanley Turrentine, Jimmy Heath, the Mingus Epitaph, Eddie Gomez and 5 Guitars Play Mingus (where he served as the primary arranger). His versatility and skill have allowed him to pair up with an array of vocal talents, from Mel Torme to Sarah Vaughan.

CHAPTER 5

Famous Country
and Folk Guitarists

Arthel 'Doc' Watson (1923 –)

Born in Deep Gap, North Carolina, Doc Watson is one of the best country-folk guitar players in American musical history. His family had a strong musical tradition, and helped foster a love of music in Watson.

An illness left Watson blind at a young age, but it could not stand in the way of his passion for music, which was insatiable. When he was ten, his father made him a fretless banjo, which he played all the time. In his early teenage years, Watson learned to play the guitar, and he and his older brother Linney began to perform traditional songs on street corners around Deep Gap.

By his late teens, Watson had learned the art of finger-picking. In 1941, he joined a band that performed regularly on a radio show in Lenoir, North Carolina. While on the show, one of the announcers called Watson 'Doc', and the nickname stuck.

In 1947, Watson married Rosa Lee Carlton, the daughter of fiddler Gaither W. Carlton. Because he was not earning very much money with his music at the time, he also worked as a piano tuner. In 1953, Watson joined the band of Jack Williams, a local pianist, as an electric guitar player. Eight years later, Watson joined the Clarence Ashley String Band and performed with them as far north as New York.

Unlike many artists of his time, Watson was middle-aged before he gained significant notoriety. The release of his first album, *The Doc Watson Family*, didn't come until 1963, when he was 40 years old. The record is a combination of folk, country and bluegrass sounds, and proved to be a powerful influence on guitar players in the early 1960s. Following on from the album, his appearances at the Newport Folk Festival in 1963 and 1964 impressed many musicians.

From 1964 , Watson recorded nearly one record a year for almost a decade. Although the folk music boom of the 1960s was eventually superseded by other styles, Watson was back in great demand in 1972, with the release of the collection called *Will the Circle Be Unbroken*, created by the Nitty Gritty Dirt Band. The guest artists included Watson, Merle Travis, Roy Acuff and a number of other country greats.

A Father and Son

Doc's son Merle Watson, who also had considerable talent, began performing with his father regularly. The result was good enough for them to win two Grammys for traditional music, in 1973 and 1974.

Father and son played together for more than 15 years, until Merle died tragically on the family farm in 1985. Following his son's death, Doc Watson continued to play publicly, wowing audiences across the nation with his abilities on the guitar (especially his flat-picking skills), and his performances of country and folk classics.

Maybelle Carter, of the seminal folk group the Carter Family – comprising Maybelle, her sister Sara and Sara's husband, A. P. Carter – played a Gibson L-5 archtop, first produced in 1922. The instrument was revolutionary, modelled on mandolins and violins, with F-shaped holes rather than one round soundhole. Maybelle's playing was sometimes described as 'church licks', and the technique was dubbed the 'Carter Scratch'.

Doc Watson is well known and respected for his command of a great many traditional American songs. He was also ahead of his time – he was an expert on the electric guitar earlier than other artists of his time. Many of Watson's fellow guitarists, such as Merle Travis and Chet Atkins, began making music on acoustic guitars and then moved to electric. Before Watson's music became successful, however, he had played the electric guitar in a small band that performed Western Swing, country and folk music. Performers such as Ricky Skaggs, Vince Gill, Clarence White and Emmylou Harris have continued to acknowledge Watson's great influence on their music.

Chet Atkins (1924–2001)

Winner of 11 Grammy awards and nine Country Music Association 'Instrumentalist of the Year' honours, Chet Atkins was the driving force behind country music's crossover into the pop charts in the late 1950s and early 1960s. As both a musician and a record producer, Atkins helped fashion the unique form of music now known as the Nashville sound.

Chet Atkins was turned on to the joy of music by both his father, a music teacher, and his brother, who played the guitar; when he was a young child, they taught him to play the fiddle. At the age of nine, he swapped his fiddle for a guitar, and the rest is history.

> Atkins faced several obstacles breaking into the music scene in the 1940s because his unique style was neither fully pop nor country.

Atkins got his first big break performing at the Grand Ole Opry supporting Red Foley in 1946. He soon became a highly popular and sought-after session player, lending his services as the studio guitarist for all RCA studio's sessions in 1949 and working with some of the most well-known musicians in the industry.

Throughout his career, Chet Atkins continued to make history, playing at the Newport Jazz Festival in 1960 and the White House in 1961, as well as recording major hits such as 'Country Gentlemen' in 1969. As a staff producer for RCA, Atkins was responsible for starting the careers of several well-known country stars, including Waylon Jennings and Charley Pride.

Throughout his career as both a musician and a producer, Chet Atkins has had a profound impact on the country music genre. His skill with the guitar and his unique ear for music and discovering new talent have made him a legend on the Nashville music scene.

Merle Travis (1917–83)

Born to a family of coal miners in Rosewood, Kentucky, Merle Travis grew up on the brink of poverty. His childhood was a great influence on his music – his hit 'Sixteen Tons' is about this mining lifestyle, incorporating a phrase that his father used to use. Travis was important in the development of rock and roll, and recorded a number of Top Ten hits and novelty songs.

Travis's first instrument was a five-string banjo, and he knew several notable teachers to help him play it. He happened to live near Ike Everly, who was later the father of Don and Phil (the Everly Brothers), and Mose Rager, who played in a unique three-finger guitar style that had developed in that part of Kentucky. These men were great influences on Travis.

As he learned more and more, Travis was able to play blues, ragtime and popular tunes. In order to earn money, Travis worked in the Civilian Conservation Corps. He also hitchhiked around the country, playing his music. In 1935, while he was visiting his brother in Indiana, Travis performed at a local dance and was recruited by local bands. This opportunity led to an appearance on a radio station, which brought him wide recognition and his big break into the music industry.

In 1937, Travis landed a broadcasting job at Cincinnati's WLW, until World War II forced it to discontinue broadcasting. Travis also amassed great popularity while performing with the Drifting Pioneers. He played a variety of music – in the late 1930s, he joined Grandpa Jones and the Delmore Brothers in a gospel quartet called the Brown's Ferry Four. While on tour with Jones, Travis visited a church in Cincinnati and heard the sermon that inspired him to write the song 'That's All'.

He served with the Marines for a short time in World War II, but was discharged and returned to Cincinnati. By early 1945 he was in Los Angeles, where he made appearances in Charles Starrett's Western films and played with Ray Whitley's Western Swing band. In 1946, he released the song 'No Vacancy', which had a particular resonance for the displaced veterans returning from World War II. The B side of 'No Vacancy' was 'Cincinnati Lou', and both quickly became hits.

Travis's next major project was a folk album, *Folk Songs of the Hills*, in 1947. The collection was released as a set of four 78 rpm records, and was considered a commercial failure at the time. However, several of Travis's best songs, including 'Sixteen Tons', 'Dark as a Dungeon', and 'Over by Number Nine', were on that collection and have become lasting successes.

Folk Songs of the Hills also contained 'Nine Pound Hammer', which incorporates an amazing acoustic solo guitar performance. Using his thumb to stop the bottom two strings allowed Travis to create mobile upper chords, teamed with jazzy voicings, open strings and rolling fast arpeggios. This style inspired generations of guitarists and helped create an instrumental style ('Travis picking') named after him.

When she was a child, Elizabeth Cotton wrote 'Freight Train', one of the most famous American folk songs. However, she didn't release her first album until she was 63, in 1958.

John Fahey (1939–2001)

Although he hated being referred to as a 'folk guitarist', John Fahey is included in this section as an easy categorization – but in reality, Fahey's legacy is far more wide-ranging. On over 40 albums, his acoustic, and later, electric, guitar compositions and playing revolutionized the role of the steel-string flat-top guitar, turning it from an accompanying instrument in folk and blues playing into a concert one, worthy of serious consideration.

Born in Takoma Park, Maryland, Fahey's first influences were bluegrass and country music, but he later claimed that the soundtrack for the 1953 Disney film, *The Thief of Baghdad*, was his first real musical ear-opener. As a young college Philosophy student, Fahey discovered the blues, inspired by a recording of 'Dark Was the Night, Cold Was the Ground' by Blind Willie Johnson, and he began to develop a unique style of finger-picking based on the great blues players, but including songsters such as Elizabeth Cotton and country players such as Sam McGee. Fahey's first recordings were 78s on the legendary Joe Buzzard's Fonotone label, under the joke name of Blind Joe Death; and 100 copies of his first, self-recorded album, *Blind Joe Death*, were issued on his own Takoma label in 1959, with one side credited to ancient blues guitarist Death and the other to his alleged protegé, Fahey. The album cost $300 to make and press, and took over three years to sell out the first pressing.

Thanks to a chance meeting at a folk festival with fellow folklorist and record collector Dick Spottiswoode, Fahey transferred to UCLA in Los Angeles to write a PhD thesis on bluesman Charley Patton. At the same time he travelled the American South to collect blues 78s, along the way 'rediscovering' the great blues singers Bukka White and Skip James. He re-recorded and issued his first album in 1964 (and again in 1967), and then, with more financial backing for his record label, began a whole series of albums through the 1960s: the sparse, blues-based compositions of the early years were joined by experiments such as 'The Great San Bernadino Birthday Party', which combined a number of performances of finger-picking and lap-slide work in open Gm tuning to make a 19-minute tone poem, and 'Requiem for Molly', on the 1967 Vanguard album *Requia*, which used found sounds and scraps of old recordings to make a soundtrack and a story.

The most immediately influential early album was *The Transfiguration of Blind Joe Death*, originally released on the tiny Riverboat label, with a hand-written booklet and a charming selection of short music-hall and blues-based pieces, which indirectly (and to Fahey's disgust) led to the New Age school of Wyndham Hill guitarists; the best-seller was *The New Possibility*, straightforward guitar renditions of Christmas hymns and carols, which sold over 250,000 copies.

By the early 1970s, Fahey's uncompromising, sometimes bleak blending of blues, country and avant-garde themes had garnered enough following for the film director Antonioni to seek him out for a soundtrack to his film *Zabriskie Point*. The project was abandoned in turmoil, save for a small fragment used in the film, but the experience led Fahey to record more ambitious and longer pieces, now often including Indian raga motifs and themes, as on *Fare Forward Voyagers* and *America* (although a similar attitude had been apparent on 'The Transcendental Waterfall', as early as the first album). At the same time, a lucrative contract with major label Reprise led to a typical piece of cussedness – instead of the two expected albums of solo 'American Primitive guitar' (as Fahey semi-seriously dubbed his music), Fahey went into the studio with top jazz and Dixieland session musicians and came out with *Of Rivers and Religion* and *After the Ball*, with a blend of his own compositions and forgotten pieces of early 20th-century Americana.

Fahey's touring and recording career continued into the late 1980s, when a bout of Epstein-Barr Disease effectively all but stopped him playing; however, he made a full recovery. In the 1990s, living in Oregon and suffering hard times, he was, in his turn, 'rediscovered' by young avant-garde and experimental musicians, and returned to performing and recording, this time on an electric guitar in a very different, minimalist style from before. His death from complications after heart surgery cut this new career short.

From Ry Cooder and Canned Heat, through Leo Kottke to Sonic Youth and Cul de Sac, the list of musicians influenced by Fahey is immense, even though they may not all experiment with open tunings, use lap slide rather than bottleneck, or wear thumb- and finger-picks; his music, based on simple themes and styles, has a subtle depth attempted by few others, and realized by fewer still.

Twelve-string guitarist Leo Kottke was inspired by classical composers such as Stravinsky, as well as bluegrass stylings. He played a Gibson B-45 12-string on his first Takoma album before changing to a Martin D-28 12-string, and then custom-built Bozo guitars with cutaways. Kottke's intense energy and crossover style incorporates open tunings and the lowest bass notes since Leadbelly, who tuned his bottom strings down two tones to C from the usual E.

Davey Graham (1942–)

Born in Leicester of Scottish and Guyanese parents, Davey Graham was one of the very first exponents of what has since become known as 'world music', his eclectic musical tastes reflecting his travels and interests, all brought together by a ground-breaking guitar style that was adopted and adapted by Paul Simon, John Martyn, Nick Drake, Bert Jansch and many others inside and outside the folk scene, including Jimmy Page of Led Zeppelin, who was also influenced by John Fahey.

In the late 1950s Graham busked throughout France, from where he travelled to North Africa and was influenced by the music of the oud, a lute variant. He returned to the UK in the early 1960s, where his appearances in London coffee bars and folk clubs became a talking point among guitarists. To play the music he was writing, Graham invented and adapted a number of open tunings, particularly DADGAD, which has become a staple for guitarists as diverse as Martin Carthy, Richard Thompson and Pierre Bensusan. After a collaborative EP with bluesman Alexis Korner, Graham's first album, *The Guitar Player*, featured his stunning takes on jazz and current pop standards, including 'Yellow Bird'; and his raga-based version of the Irish traditional tune 'She Moved Thro' the Fair' came out on another EP, *From a London Hootenanny*, in 1963.

In 1964 Graham released *Folk, Blues and Beyond* on the Decca label, which turned out to be his most influential recording, mixing and blending Leadbelly, folksinger Cyril Tawney, jazzman Bobby Timmons and further adventures into Indian classical stylings, all on a steel-string Gibson guitar; a whole generation of British acoustic guitarists sat and listened in awe. The following year, Graham's collaboration with English folk singer Shirley Collins on British folk songs, *Folk Roots, New Routes*, was not as successful, but its legacy has lasted well.

Graham's later 1960s albums included *Midnight Man*, *Large as Life and Twice as Natural* and *Hat*, but his insistence on reworking the tunes of others into his own repertoire, rather than composing original material, and an increasing reliance on drugs and general unreliability, led to a semi-retirement from recording and performing until the late 1970s, when *The Complete Guitarist* and *Dance for Two People* were magnificent returns to form: sarod and oud joined the guitar on everything from Orlando Gibbons and J.S. Bach through to Seamus Ennis, Horace Silver and Vaughan Williams. Since then, Graham has spent most of his time teaching guitar in North London, with frequent visits to North Africa and beyond, and has appeared on a handful of tracks on compilation albums. His low profile and somewhat diffident persona denied him major sales and widespread fame, but his influence is immense.

CHAPTER 6

Famous
Rock and Pop
Guitarists

Chuck Berry (1926–)

Chuck Berry's manic, fast guitar work and pop genius songwriting have been the source of inspiration for such acts as the Beatles and the Rolling Stones. He has played with everyone from Bruce Springsteen to Tina Turner to Keith Richards. Reading a list of his hits is like reading Chapter 1 of the guitar rock bible: 'Sweet Little Sixteen', 'Roll Over Beethoven' and his masterpiece, 'Johnny B. Goode'.

Berry went from singing in a Baptist church to transforming American music. He fused blues, country and R&B styles, blending together pieces of America's musical puzzle to create a loud, suggestive, totally original form of music called rock and roll. He put the focus on the guitar-wielding front man with his fast-paced live performances, appealing to audiences of all colours – especially young people.

One of the true originators of rock and roll, Chuck Berry was the first artist to be inducted into the Rock and Roll Hall of Fame.

Eric Clapton (1945–)

Clapton is the most prominent rock guitarist to have emerged from England since the 1960s. At an early age, his style showed the influences of bluesmen like Big Bill Broonzy, Robert Johnson and Muddy Waters. The Rock and Roll Hall of Fame credits his version of J. J. Cale's song 'After Midnight' as being instrumental in shaping rock and roll history.

In 1963, Clapton joined the seminal R&B group the Yardbirds. Two years later, he left the band because they had become too 'pop' in his opinion, making room for two more guitarists who would become superstars, Jeff Beck and Jimmy Page.

Clapton next joined John Mayall's Bluesbreakers (Mick Fleetwood, John McVie and Peter Green, the nucleus of Fleetwood Mac, also played with Mayall), and in 1966, he returned to London to form Cream with bass player Jack Bruce and drummer Ginger Baker.

Cream broke up in 1968, and Clapton and Ginger Baker hooked up with Steve Winwood in a band called Blind Faith. This didn't last long either, and Clapton next appeared at the Rock 'n' Roll Revival Show in Toronto as a member of John Lennon's Plastic Ono Band.

In 1970, Clapton formed his own band, Derek and the Dominos. He fell in love with Patti Harrison, the wife of his good friend George Harrison, and his feelings for Patti inspired the now-classic song 'Layla'. (He eventually caused Patti and George's divorce, after which he himself married and then divorced Patti.) Clapton retired from the music business for a while, incapacitated by a drug problem.

In 1990, Clapton won a Billboard Music Award for Top Album Rock Artist, but also lost several members of his road crew and his friend Stevie Ray Vaughan in a helicopter crash. In 1991 Clapton won a Grammy Award for Best Rock Vocal Male (his first solo Grammy) for 'Bad Love'. In 1993, Clapton won six Grammy Awards for his *Unplugged* album.

Jimi Hendrix (1942–70)

One of the greatest rock guitarists of all time, Hendrix outshone his contemporaries, reinventing the sound and concept of playing the electric guitar. Born in Seattle, Washington, he was drawn to blues and rock through radio and records. He got his first guitar at the age of 12 and was playing with local bands by the time he was 16. After serving in Vietnam during the early 1960s, he turned professional in 1962.

Hendrix was a sideman for a number of R&B artists, such as Little Richard, Ike and Tina Turner, and the Isley Brothers, but he was frustrated by not having the opportunity to use his talents fully, so he set out solo. He moved to New York in 1965, playing in bars and clubs, and put together his first band, called Jimmy James and the Blue Flames. Chas Chandler, the bass player for the Animals, met Hendrix one night at a club in Greenwich Village. After hearing Hendrix play, Chas talked him into moving to London to work with him.

Rise to Fame

Hendrix arrived in London in September 1966, with Chandler as his manager. An extraordinary guitarist and spectacular showman, Hendrix was an immediate sensation. Hendrix and Chandler brought in drummer Mitch Mitchell and bassist Noel Redding to form the Jimi Hendrix Experience. They played their first live concerts in France before going into the studio to record.

The music of the Experience combined R&B and soul into a new sound that became the epitome of psychedelia, which was just becoming the signature fashion of the late 1960s. Hendrix's debut single was 'Hey Joe'.

During the recording session Hendrix met Roger Mayer, an electronics engineer who had developed new sound effects for the guitar. These effects can be heard on the next single, 'Purple Haze'.

Jimi Hendrix played left-handed on a standard right-hand model Fender Stratocaster – as well as a Gibson Flying V and a Les Paul – upside down, though the guitar was strung in the traditional way, but tuned down a semitone. Hendrix's main amplifiers were Marshall 100-watt models with two four-by-twelve cabinets, and he often used a fuzz pedal, a wah-wah, an Octavia and a Uni-vibe built or modified by Roger Mayer.

Hendrix really exploded onto the scene with his debut album, *Are You Experienced?* (1967), which he followed up with *Axis: Bold As Love* later that year. Both albums took Hendrix's guitar playing and songwriting to new levels. His singles hit the Top Ten in the UK, resulting in an invitation to a spot in the Monterey Pop Festival in the USA later that year.

Drawing on the R&B showmanship of his early years, Hendrix captured the attention of the audience with his on-stage drama – playing the guitar behind his back, with his teeth and even above his head. One of his set's highlights was 'Wild Thing', when he smashed his guitar against amplifiers to generate atonal chords before pouring lighter fluid over the instrument, setting it on fire and smashing it to pieces, stunning his audience.

Experimentation

Crowds and audiences, inside and outside the music industry, were captivated by Hendrix's experimentation. To get his music across to the crowd, he used distorted riffs, mind-blowing feedback and thumping wah-wah sound effects.

In 1969 he played the Woodstock festival with an extended lineup that included Billy Cox, who replaced Noel Redding on bass. The performance was electrifying (and was captured on film), and climaxed with an anti-Vietnam War version of 'The Star-Spangled Banner', filled with screeching avant-garde notes and feedback, that became a grotesque parody of the original and a highly charged political statement.

Hendrix formed a new group, the Band of Gypsies, which recorded one album in 1970, a live recording of their debut concert at the Filmore East in New York. After that, Hendrix recorded only one more album – the double LP *Electric Ladyland* – before he died of an accidental drug overdose in 1970 at the age of 27.

During the five years or so that he was active in the studio, Hendrix also experimented with funk, jazz and Mississippi Delta blues, but never released another official album. After his death, producers collected some of these tracks and released them on compilation albums.

In July 1995, Hendrix's father, Al Hendrix, won control of Jimi's estate and enlisted Jimi's sister, Janie Hendrix-Wright to help him put together a video of the making of *Electric Ladyland*.

Frank Zappa (1940–93)

While Hendrix was arguably the most talented player, Zappa was probably the most sophisticated and imaginative composer of the 1960s rock scene.

Born in Baltimore, Zappa grew up in California. He began in music by playing drums, and his heightened percussive and rhythmic sense can be heard woven through all his guitar playing. He joined a band called the Soul Giants in 1964. The following year they transformed themselves into the Mothers of Invention, and in 1966 they released their first LP, *Freak Out*. The album introduced the intense and emotional world of rock and roll to Zappa's sardonic humour, penchant for creating pastiches of popular styles, and avant-garde musical experimentation.

From the start, Zappa tried to expand the musical language of rock by blending in modern classical and jazz-influenced harmony, odd time signatures, exotic instruments and studio techniques such as editing, overdubbing and tape manipulation. He developed a way of playing the guitar in long, directional solos with effects, expanding organically with his rhythmic and melodic ideas. Zappa created highly innovative material that has both quality and depth, before his death from cancer.

Robert Fripp (1946–)

The music of Robert Fripp has enthralled and dazzled audiences and fans for more than 30 years. His willingness to explore the edges of rock music and push experimental new music ideas have made him an icon in the music world.

Fripp was born in Dorset, where he began to learn to play the guitar at the age of 11. His career as a musician began in the 1960s, when he played with a band called the League of Gentlemen. After a while, he auditioned for a band being formed by brothers Peter and Mike Giles, and the three of them became the trio Giles, Giles and Fripp, but they recorded only one album, in 1968, entitled *The Cheerful Insanity of Giles, Giles and Fripp*, before they disbanded.

A Turn of Luck

However, Fripp found fame and fortune in his next endeavour – a band called King Crimson (which Mike Giles also joined). Their debut album, *In the Court of the Crimson King*, which came out in 1969, set the stage in establishing Crimson's place at the top of the progressive rock world. The band combined Hendrix-influenced rock, improvisation and classical jazz to make their own dynamic sound that resonated with audiences. However, the band suffered the comings and goings of various members over the next five years, until Fripp finally broke up the band in 1974.

During this time, Fripp had been playing music with musician Brian Eno, who introduced him to a new interactive tape technology that would loop endlessly, repeating the notes the performer played, a trick that resulted in a harmonic accompaniment that they dubbed 'Frippertronics'. The two together recorded two albums, *No Pussyfooting* (1973) and *Evening Star* (1975).

Fripp began working on his first solo album in the late 1970s, releasing *Exposure* in 1979, which included a mix of music influenced by the emerging punk and urban-blues styles. In 1981 he began working with a new band, and resurrected the King Crimson name long enough to record three albums – *Discipline, Three Of A Perfect Pair* and *Beat* – before disbanding in 1984.

In the mid-1980s, Fripp developed a travelling guitar workshop, the League of Crafty Guitarists, to teach his methods of discipline and practice. He has produced three albums from these workshops.

King Crimson was revived again in the 1990s, releasing *Vrooom* (1994) and *Thrak* (1995), and is still together today. Fripp has also kept up his solo exploration of experimental music, producing the *Soundscape* series of albums in the mid-1990s, and *A Temple in the Clouds* in 2000.

Jimmy Page (1944–)

When the bands Deep Purple and Led Zeppelin formed in 1968, a new style of hard rock emerged. Blending elements of blues, rock, classical guitar and jazz, along with heavy use of powered amps and sound effects, the new sound quickly took the world by storm.

Jimmy Page, born in Heston, Middlesex, emerged as a guitar superstar in this new sound. Page performed and recorded in London in his early years. In 1966 he joined the Yardbirds. Less than three years later, the quartet split because of artistic differences. Page then formed the New Yardbirds, a hard-rock group that was formed to fulfill the original Yardbirds' contractual obligations.

Led Zeppelin Is Born

The New Yardbirds changed their name to Led Zeppelin shortly after, and became one of the most popular groups of the 1970s. Page came to be regarded as one of the most talented guitarists in popular music. In addition to his guitar work, Page also produced Led Zeppelin's albums, controlling much of the band's sound.

Where did the band name Led Zeppelin come from?
Keith Moon, the drummer for the Who, came up with a name when he made a joke about the new band crashing like a lead zeppelin. Later, 'lead' was changed to 'led' to ensure that the name would be said correctly.

After the band broke up in the early 1980s, Page went on to record with a new quartet called The Firm, which released two Top Thirty albums in 1985 and 1986. In 1988, Page released his solo debut, *Outrider*, on Geffen Records; the album included appearances by former Led Zeppelin singer Robert Plant and Jason Bonham, Zeppelin drummer John Bonham's son.

In the 1990s, Page reunited with Plant for an *MTV Unplugged* show. The pair performed various classic Zeppelin tracks with a world music twist. Some of the songs from that ended up on 1994's *No Quarter*, which was promoted with a world tour.

Page and the Black Crowes got together in 1999 for a concert in England that led to a US tour. Following that success, the new partners recorded an album called *Jimmy Page and the Black Crowes Live at the Greek*. Page continues to record and perform today.

Jeff Beck (1944–)

Along with Eric Clapton and Jimi Hendrix, Jeff Beck is considered one of the best guitarists of his time. A versatile and highly skilled guitarist, Beck may not have received the same sort of media attention as Clapton and Hendrix, but he still boasts of millions of fans worldwide.

Beck was born in Wallington, Surrey. He attended art school in London, but spent much of his time in music, performing with various local bands. After playing with the controversial Screaming Lord Sutch, Beck's reputation grew, and in 1965 the Yardbirds asked him to join them after their then guitarist, Eric Clapton, decided to leave.

Beck was with the blues-rock group for about a year and a half, maintaining their success in the charts. At the end of 1966, Beck left the Yardbirds to start a solo career. With Rod Stewart on vocals, Ron Wood on bass and Aynsley Dunbar at drums, the quartet formed the Jeff Beck Group. They released their debut LP, *Truth*, in 1968, and had a massive hit with 'Hi Ho Silver Lining'.

In 1970, Rod Stewart and Ron Wood left the Jeff Beck Group and joined the Faces. Beck reformed the group with vocalist Bobby Tench, bassist Clive Chapman, keyboardist Max Middleton and drummer Cozy Powell. In 1973 he formed a new trio with former Vanilla Fudge/Cactus members Tim Bogart (bass) and Carmine Appice (drums).

In 1975 came *Blow by Blow*. This album, produced by Beatles' producer George Martin, was more experimental than those in Beck's past, with an instrumental jazz-fusion flavour. The following year, Beck teamed up with former Mahavishnu Orchestra keyboardist Jan Hammer to put out *Wired*, which was successful.

Over the next decade, Beck did a lot more collaborative work and then took a break from the music world for a while. Finally in 1985, he came out with *Flash*, which was to become one of his most commercially successful albums.

In 1987, Beck appeared on Mick Jagger's album *Primitive Cool*. Two years later he released an all-instrumental album, *Guitar Shop*, which won a Grammy for Best Rock Instrumental. In 1999, Beck released his first album of original material, entitled *Who Else!*, a collection of 11 new guitar compositions in various styles. His most recent album, *You Had It Coming*, came out in 2001.

CHAPTER 7

How to Find
and Buy a Guitar

Finding What's Right for You

Choosing and buying a guitar is a fairly important step in learning how to play. By far the best thing you can do is take along a friend or teacher who plays the guitar, and ask them to help you. This won't always be possible, of course, so you're going to have to learn how to find a good guitar for yourself unaided.

In general, don't buy an instrument on your first visit to a music shop. Test lots of different types of guitars, and visit lots of music shops more than once before you make a decision on your instrument.

Coming up with a plan now that defines your ideas about music doesn't mean you can't change your mind later on. This isn't do or die – here, it's just a place to start. To begin, you'll want to consider issues such as type, expense, appearance, construction, neck and action, which are covered next.

Types of Guitars

There are three main types of guitar to consider: classical, acoustic (and acoustic-electric) steel string and solid-body electric. What you buy largely depends on the kind of music you like to listen to and want to learn to play for yourself.

If you're not sure exactly what you want to learn, or if you want to learn to play a number of styles, you should choose either a classical or 'folk' (acoustic) guitar. A classical guitar uses nylon strings, which are a little easier on your left-hand fingertips (assuming you're right-handed), although the neck is a little wider than on a folk guitar. A folk guitar has steel strings, which are a little harder on your fingertips at first, but it has a narrower neck.

Learning to play an acoustic instrument – 'unplugged' in effect – is cheaper and easier than going straight in for an electric guitar and amplifier, which could prove to be more expensive and complicated. Once you have some familiarity with the instrument, you'll know better which kind you want to learn to play next.

There are lots of different types of guitars made for the many different kinds of music you can play. If you go into a music shop and say you're looking for a guitar to play Eric Clapton-like rock blues, the shop owner will show you a solid-bodied electric based on a Fender Stratocaster or a Gibson Les Paul. Say that you want to play jazz guitar like Emily Remler or Johnny Smith, and the salesperson will bring you an F-hole, hollow-bodied cello acoustic guitar along the lines of the Gibson ES-175 or Gibson Super 400.

For blues and R&B, the guitar of choice is based on a Gibson ES-335 or ES-355. If your passion is folk music and your hero is Jewel, Nick Drake or early Bob Dylan, go for a steel-string acoustic. If you want to play classical or flamenco, start on a nylon-string guitar.

The truth is, however, that you can play anything on any kind of guitar. What counts is not the kind of guitar you have, but what's in your head. The best advice is to keep it simple. Remember, even 'wild men' like Jimi Hendrix, Chuck Berry and Steve Vai could play acoustic guitar as well as they could play electric.

Expense

First things first: money. Buying cheap is not necessarily the best idea, though you don't have to spend thousands of pounds on an instrument and equipment, either. Don't put yourself into debt, but be aware that you should think in terms of at least £120 to £250. You can easily spend £500 and a lot more if you're not careful.

The more expensive the guitar is, the better (and more seductive) it seems to be. You need to try to balance the 'new toy' syndrome with a realistic understanding of what you can afford, and what you need to learn to play well. Play a really expensive guitar and compare it to a much cheaper model. What differences do you notice?

Unless you are working as a musician and you're buying yourself a new tool of the trade, don't spend too much. It won't be worth it.

Used and Secondhand Instruments

Is it a good idea to buy a used or secondhand guitar? Certainly. While a new guitar has to be broken in and can take up to six months to 'wake up', a used guitar in good condition is already 'alive' and could be a bargain.

You can expect to pay as much as 40 per cent less than the list price for a used guitar (unless it's a classic of some sort), depending on where you get it. Compare the prices in music shops, pawnbrokers and newspaper ads, and gather as much knowledge and information as you can.

Mail-Order Guitars

Is it a good idea to buy a guitar through a mail order or over the Internet? Not really. Just like buying a car, you need to 'test-drive' the instrument, making sure that you're comfortable with it and that it works. Just knowing the make and model isn't a guarantee that a particular instrument is worth buying, or worth the money that people are asking for it.

Call a music shop or check catalogues for specific model prices. A Gibson Les Paul sells for approximately £1,500, but a good copy can cost £300. A Fender Stratocaster costs around £750 (but copies can be only £100), and a decent nylon-string classical guitar can be bought for under £200.

Aesthetics/Appearance

A blue guitar does not inherently play better than a red or blonde one. Of course, what your new 'partner' looks like is important in terms of your desire to spend a lot of time with it. But that said, never buy a guitar on looks alone.

Construction

With an acoustic guitar, gently tap the top and back of the instrument to make sure nothing rattles. (You're listening for loose struts inside.) Look inside the sound hole for glue spills and other signs of sloppy workmanship. Check that all the pieces of wood join together smoothly, and that there are no gaps between pieces.

An acoustic guitar's sound is principally made by the top – the back and sides reflect and amplify the sound. So a solid-wood acoustic guitar is preferable to a laminated-wood guitar (where the manufacturer presses together layers of inexpensive wood and covers the top layer with veneer). However, solid-wood guitars can be very expensive, and laminated-wood guitars can be pretty good. They are sometimes stronger than solid-wood guitars; the lamination process results in a stronger (though less acoustically responsive) wood.

With electric guitars, make sure that knobs, wires and other metal parts are secure and rattle-free. Strum the open strings strongly and listen for rattles. A solid-body guitar is basically an electric instrument with no real acoustic sound. The wood that it's made from is irrelevant. It is all electrics. So make sure the pickups and wiring are in good working order. There should be no hum or cutting out, and the volume and tone controls should all work without crackles and other noises.

Another important consideration is how long the note will sustain. To check this, you need to use an amplifier for best results. Fret a note and play it. Don't use an open string, and don't move the string, just keep fretting the note until it fades away. Why bother with this? Well, a good sustain period is four seconds or more, which means the guitar will be good for playing fusion and rock. It also means the guitar is in good order. If the sustain is less than four seconds, then it's a questionable instrument and you should think twice about buying it. Bear in mind, however, that this doesn't necessarily make it a bad instrument. There could be a number of reasons why the sustain is not longer. If the guitar is otherwise a bargain, this problem might be easily fixed by a guitar repairer. Get a professional to check the instrument before you make a final decision. The lack of sustain could be something as simple as a bridge that is out of alignment or a nut that needs to be filed properly, or it may be just that the strings are old or simply not good.

It can often be the right thing for a first-time electric guitar buyer to buy a Squier Stratocaster or an Epiphone Les Paul copy instead of the 'real thing'. The difference in price is huge (see opposite), and the differences in quality and play are subtle.

Neck

Pick up the guitar by the head and peer down the neck to make sure it's not warped. Does the guitar have a truss rod? Most guitars now come with one, but make sure this one does. Does the neck bolt on? You can usually see where the neck is attached at the heel with a heel plate, under which are four or five bolts. Fender Stratocasters and Telecasters have bolt-on necks. Is the neck glued on? Classical guitars and Gibson Les Pauls have glued necks, where it looks as though the neck and the body are made from one piece of wood.

Run your fingers along the edge of the neck to make sure the fret wire doesn't need filing or reseating. The fret wire should be seated well on the fingerboard, and the ends should not be loose or feel jagged. Is the neck made from ebony, rosewood or maple? Cheaper guitars use mahogany or plywood stained black or rust red. The more expensive guitars with better fingerboards are worth the money. Are the notes at the bottom of the neck in tune? Are they as easy to play as the notes at the top of the fingerboard? Do any of the notes have a buzzing sound, even though you're stopping them properly? Is the intonation accurate? Do the notes on the 12th fret correspond to the harmonics at the same place? The notes may have different tonal qualities, but they should have the pitch. Pay attention to the third and sixth strings in particular. On a guitar that's not set up well or has a problem, these strings may be hard to keep in tune.

If you don't trust your own knowledge or ears, enlist the help of an experienced guitarist. It's vital to make sure you don't buy something that's going to be really hard to play.

Action

The instrument's 'action' or playability is determined by the setting of the string over and between the bridge (at the bottom of the guitar) and the nut (just before the tuning heads). Setting and adjusting these two things is a real art, but the strings shouldn't be so low that the notes buzz when they are played, nor so high that the strings need a lot of physical strength to be held down. If the notes are hard to play or out of tune, get someone in the shop to adjust the instrument. If they can't – or won't – fix the instrument, don't buy it.

A Second Guitar

If you're thinking of buying a second guitar, don't go crazy. You should have reached the stage where you realize the limitations of your current instrument, and you should have a much more precise idea of what you want to do with your next one In general, go for an instrument that is a little more expensive than the one you have at present, or that gives you more range and flexibility to explore different music sounds and styles, such as a 12-string or an electric guitar and amplifier.

In the Shop

We can practically guarantee that the salesperson's first question for you will be, 'How much do you want to spend?'

Know the answer. It will save the two of you a lot of time and aggravation. Almost certainly, the next topic of conversation will involve what kind of music you want to play on the instrument (there's no point noodling around on a Fender Stratocaster and waxing lyrical about Paco Peña and flamenco), and what level of technical accomplishment you've reached on the instrument.

Listen carefully to what the salesperson has to say, and don't be rushed into a sale. After the sales pitch, say, 'Thanks, I'd like to think about it.' Then leave the shop and at least have a cup of coffee before you decide to return and plunk down your hard-earned cash. Ideally, go to another store and go through the process again. Listen for differences in what the two salespeople have to say to you about the same subjects.

Tips for Buying a Guitar

- Buy quality when possible, but don't overspend.
- Enjoy the instrument. Fall in love, if you can. Finding the right guitar is like meeting the woman (or man) of your dreams. There's an immediate 'simpatico' or magnetism that is inexplicable, but nevertheless real.
- Check the fingerboard for warping. Look down the neck as if sighting down a rifle barrel. It's normal to see slight curving around the seventh fret, which can be adjusted using the truss rod, but if the neck looks twisted, don't buy it.
- Check the intonation. The 12th fret should always be exactly one octave higher than the open string.
- Check the action. Look at the distance between the nut and the bridge. A low action means the strings are closer to the frets, so your fingers don't have to work as hard to press the strings to the fingerboard. Listen for buzzes and rattles.
- Check the tuning heads. If they turn too easily the strings may slip, making the guitar difficult to keep in tune.
- Check the sustain on each note. Sustain is the length of time a note rings out. Play every note on the fretboard to make sure all the notes sustain equally.
- If you're buying an electric guitar, check the pickups. Make sure each string has the same volume level. Significant differences can indicate that the pole (or screw beneath each string) may need to be adjusted. If not, the whole pickup may need to be replaced.
- Check for noise. With the guitar plugged in, stand it close to an amplifier and listen. Whistling or feedback might suggest that the pickups aren't well isolated, and it could be a problem playing the guitar at high volume. Make sure the amplifier in the shop is not masking faults with the guitar you're playing.

CHAPTER 8

How to Tune,
Care for and Maintain
Your Guitar

Anatomy of a Guitar

If you look at FIGURE 1(a) opposite, you'll see that a guitar has three basic parts: a body, a neck and a head.

Body

The body is where the sound comes from in an acoustic guitar. It consists of a top piece, which is a sounding board with a soundhole, and a back and sides, which contain the sound and make it resonate.

In a purely electric guitar, the body is made of a solid piece of wood to avoid feedback, or too much resonance or screeching when the sound is amplified. It also houses the electronic pickups (which convert the motion of the strings into an electronic signal that can be sent through an amplifier of some kind), and volume and tone controls (which vary the loudness and bass and treble frequencies of the signal). There is also a socket called an output jack, into which you insert a special plug or jack. The other end of the jack goes into a corresponding socket in an amplifier.

In addition, the body has a bridge, made from either wood or metal, which anchors the strings. There are also strap pins or posts, which you can use to attach a shoulder strap.

Neck

The neck is usually fixed to the body by bolts or glue, or formed from the body in one piece. It often has a metal truss rod running through it to strengthen it and help adjust any slight warping or twisting. The neck has a flat piece of wood (usually mahogany or ebony) called the fingerboard or fretboard. The fingerboard is divided into sections called frets. These sections are marked off by pieces of wire set into the wood, called fret wire. By stopping a string in between the fret wires – that is, in the middle of the fret – the frets determine the different pitches or notes you can make on each string. The strings run from the bridge, along the neck and across the nut – which is a piece of wood, plastic or metal at the top of the neck with slight grooves for each of the six strings – to the tuning pegs.

FIGURE 1(a):
Acoustic guitar

Headstock

Tuning pegs

Nut

Frets

Neck

Fingerboard

Soundhole/sound chamber

Finger plate
(pick guard)

Body

Bridge

Top (sounding board)

FIGURE 1(b):
Electric guitar

Headstock

Tuning pegs

Nut

Frets

Fingerboard

Neck

Body

Front pickup
(for rhythm)

Back pickup
(for lead)

Bridge

Tailpiece

Electric lead
socket

Tone & volume
controls

End pin

Head

The head, sometimes called a headstock, holds the tuning pegs (also called tuning machines, machine heads or tuning gears) that the strings are attached to. On a six-string guitar there are six tuning pegs. Each tuning peg has a knob you can turn using your fingers. The knob will tighten or loosen the string tension and thus put each string into tune.

There are three bass strings and three treble strings. (More about strings appears later.)

How it all Works

The principle of the guitar is simple. A string is stretched at high tension across the fingerboard between the tuning peg and either the bridge or the tailpiece. By using a fingertip to stop the string at various places on the fingerboard, and plucking the string near the soundhole, you can make the string produce a variety of pitches, or notes. The shorter the length of string, the higher the pitch; the longer the string, the lower the pitch. (That's why a double bass has a booming bass sound, and a mandolin or violin has a more high-pitched, treble sound.)

As with string length, string thickness also affects pitch. The thinner the string, the higher the pitch. In addition to the length of the string affecting whether you get a high note (short length = treble) or a low note (long length = bass), the strings range in thickness. The thinnest is the E string 1 (treble) and the thickest is the E string 6 (bass). (This is all elementary physics and acoustics if you want to delve into the science of the thing. We won't bother here.) The gauge of a string refers to its thickness. So you can have the same pitch on, say, the E string 1, but use different gauges of string to achieve the same result.

By angling the bridge correctly, you change the string length and therefore help create the right pitch. You add to this by using strings of varying thickness, called gauges, which are measured in millimetres.

What's the advantage of having, say, an E string 1 that is a thin gauge? The answer is that the string is more easily bendable and therefore works better for certain types of playing. You don't want heavy-gauge strings for rock playing, but light gauge. For jazz you would use a heavier gauge. For example, Steve Vai probably uses a .009 or .010 string 1, while jazz guitarist Pat Martino might use a .013 or higher for his first string.

The principle of the guitar is simple. A string is stretched at high tension across the fingerboard between the tuning peg and the bridge. By using a fingertip to stop the string at various places on the fingerboard, and plucking the string near the soundhole, you can make the string produce a variety of pitches, or notes.

Each fret on the guitar is a 'half-step' away from the fret on either side. A half-step is the smallest interval, or distance between two notes, you can have in Western music. If you look at a piano keyboard, you'll see it's mostly made up of alternating black notes and white notes that are half-steps away from each other.

On the guitar, to play two notes a half-step away from each other, all you have to do is stop any string in the middle of a fret, and then stop that string in the middle of the next fret. So to go up or down the guitar in half-steps, all you have to do is move your finger up or down the strings, stopping the strings one fret at a time.

Electric guitars have added elements. Just like an acoustic guitar, shortening or lengthening a string will give you a variety of pitches, or notes. But there's a problem: without a hollow body that resonates, where does the sound come from?

The sound comes from electronic pickups, wire-wrapped magnets that act like tiny microphones placed under each string. The vibrations of the string cause the magnet in a pickup to resonate (or, more accurately, to 'modulate') a tiny magnetic field. That signal is picked up by the pickup and turned into a small electrical current. In turn, that current is conducted from the pickup to an external amplifier by an electrical cable that has one end plugged into the guitar and the other into an amplifier. How loud the note is – and whether it's distorted, thick and bassy, or thin and trebly – is all determined by volume, tone and effects controls on both the guitar and the amplifier.

Tuning the Guitar

A joke goes that a beginner guitarist spent nearly £2,000 on a new Gibson Les Paul. He proudly went along for his first music lesson, and almost boastfully asked the teacher to try out the guitar, sure that the teacher would praise such an excellent purchase.

The teacher strummed a few chords, and then said, 'It's a bit out of tune. We should have a lesson on how to tune it.'

Angrily, the student said, 'Are you kidding me? That guitar cost me a fortune. What a rip-off! It was definitely in tune when I bought it in the music shop!'

Care and maintenance of your instrument is an important and normal part of learning to play the guitar (or any instrument). Keeping the strings in tune, and even changing them on a regular basis, is important if you want to get the best from your guitar.

Unless you're going to make a habit of treating guitars like Jimi Hendrix or Pete Townsend, who climaxed their stage acts by smashing and burning their instruments (not recommended!), don't drop your new guitar, or scratch it. However, changing strings and tuning your guitar is recommended (highly) if you want to get the most from it.

There are lots of ways of tuning your guitar, and lots of types of tunings you can experiment with. However, for the moment we're going to concentrate on only one tuning – the standard, 'concert' tuning. The thickest bass note is called string 6, and the strings are tuned as follows:

String 6: E

String 5: A

String 4: D

String 3: G

String 2: B

String 1: E

Note that the top string (1) and the bottom string (6) are tuned to the same note, but two octaves apart.

Strings 6, 5 and 4 are the bass strings. Strings 3, 2 and 1 are the treble strings. String 6 is the thickest; string 1 is the thinnest.

Try to memorize the names of the open strings. Once again, they are E, A, D, G, B and E. Make up a phrase starting with each letter so you can easily recall the string names.

FIGURE 2(a):

**Open strings
and notes on
the fifth fret**

FIGURE 2(b):
The open guitar string notes on a keyboard

MIDDLE C

E 6　A 5　D 4　G 3　B 2　E 1

Relative Tuning

The easiest way to tune your guitar if you're playing alone is called relative tuning. That means the guitar is in tune relative to itself, although not necessarily to other instruments. You can tune the guitar from any string, but usually you start from string 6, the E bass string.

To begin, count up five frets – that is, five spaces between the fret wires (see FIGURE 2(a)) – on string 6. Then use your first fingertip on your left hand to stop the string at this fret and play the note. This is the note A. Now play string 5 while the note on string 6 is still sounding. (Make sure to play string 5 'open', without stopping it at any frets.) Listen for the 'wow-wow-wow' sound the two strings make as they sound together. Is the note of string 5 higher or lower than the note of string 6? If it is higher, then you are sharp. Turn the tuning peg on string 5 to lower the sound of the note. If it is lower, then you are flat. Turn the tuning peg until the note sounds higher.

Keep playing both strings at the same time, or one string immediately after the other, so that both notes are sounding at the same time. If you're not sure, keep lowering the note on the open string until it is obviously too low, then try raising it again. The closer you get to being in tune, the more the 'wow-wow-wow' sound will slow down and eventually disappear. When it disappears completely, you're in tune. Just get it as close as you can for the moment.

Next, stop string 5 at the fifth fret and play the note there. (The note is D.) Play string 4 open at the same time. Again, adjust the open string using the tuning peg until both strings are sounding the same note.

Next, stop string 4 at the fifth fret and play the note there (G). Play string 3 open at the same time. Again, adjust the open string using the tuning peg until both strings are sounding the same note.

Tuning string 2 is slightly different. Stop string 3 at the *fourth* fret and play the note there (B). Play string 2 open at the same time. Again, adjust the open string using the tuning peg until both strings are sounding the same note.

Next, stop string 2 at the fifth fret and play the note there (E). Play string 1 open at the same time. Again, adjust the open string using the tuning peg until both strings are sounding the same note.

If the strings are new, they may slip a little bit. Tuning is about constant adjustment. So don't be afraid to go back and try to adjust the strings already in tune to make sure they haven't gone out of tune a little bit.

Other Ways to Tune a Guitar

Here are some other things you can do to make sure the strings are in tune with each other:

Play string 1 and string 6 together. They're both E strings, remember (although two octaves apart). Try to make sure they sound the same note.

Play notes an octave apart. To do this, stop string 5 at the seventh fret. This sounds the note E. Now play string 6 (E) open at the same time. Make the adjustment to the higher-pitched, fretted string. The two notes are an octave apart. Do the same on the other strings. Remember, on string 3 stop the string at the eighth fret and play string 2 open to sound the note B. Then play string 2 at the seventh fret and string 1 open.

Match octaves by playing every other string. Again, make the adjustment to the higher-pitched, fretted string. Play string 6 (E) open, then stop string 4 at the second fret (E) and sound that note at the same time. Then match string 5 (A) open with string 3 stopped at the second fret. Play string 4 (D) open, with string 2 stopped at the third fret. Play string 3 (G) open with string 1 stopped at the third fret.

Get into the habit of making sure your guitar is in tune every time you pick it up to play.

Tuning Using Harmonics

This is a complicated subject. For now, just accept the following. If you lightly touch a string over the fret wire on the 12th fret with a finger while gently plucking close to the bridge, you will get a note called a harmonic.

Following the same 'light touch' technique, play the harmonic on string 6 at the fifth fret (E), followed by the harmonic on string 5 at the seventh fret. Adjust string 5 until it's in tune.

Compare harmonics on string 5, fifth fret (A), and then string 4, seventh fret. Adjust string 4 if necessary.

Compare harmonics on string 4, fifth fret (D) with string 3, seventh fret. Adjust string 3.

Compare harmonics on string 6, seventh fret (B) with string 2, 12th fret. Adjust string 2.

Compare harmonics on string 5, seventh fret (E) with string 1, 12th fret. Adjust string 1.

Strum a chord, such as G, A minor or E, one string at a time (arpeggio style), and then together, and listen to the strings working in harmony with each other. Bear in mind that a string may sound out of tune in one chord, and work well in another.

Tuning takes practice and patience, but it's important that you master it.

Tuning to a Reference Source

We've looked at tuning the guitar to itself, but what do you do if you're playing with other musicians and your guitar is out of tune with them? Well, you tune to a fixed source. You can use pitch pipes, a tuning fork or an electronic tuner that will help you put each string into 'concert' pitch. (This is the term for commonly accepted pitches that everyone uses, regardless of their instrument.) You can even find music software programs (some of them are free or shareware on the Internet) that will give you the correct pitch for your strings.

A tuning fork is tuned to concert A, below middle C. Strike the fork until it hums, then place the leg of the fork against the body of the guitar near the bridge so you can hear it resonate. Then, while the fork is sounding, play string 5 open (A) and listen for the pulsing until the string is in tune.

Strings

Strings don't last forever. In fact, depending how much you play and practise, and whether you live in a hot climate or not, you could change your strings as often as once a week. In general, however, once every eight to 12 weeks is about average. If a string breaks, it's probably time to change the whole set, rather than just replace the one that broke. Strings lose their stretch and vibrancy over time because of salt from sweaty fingers and rust. You can also find a variety of problems with bridges and nuts, and so forth, which are discussed later on.

You can extend the life of your strings by cleaning them after each session. To get rid of the gunge under the string, some players 'snap' each string by pulling it back slightly, as if the string is on a bow, and then snapping it back to the fingerboard.

Here's a trick used by string bass players: take off the strings and boil them in water for ten minutes or so. This removes grease and gunge. However, replacing treble strings in particular can be a pain – it's better to just bite the bullet and get a new set of strings.

Strings come in a variety of gauges. The thicknesses are described in fractions of an inch. Choosing a gauge of string is very much a personal decision.

In general, the lighter the string gauge, the easier it is to bend and hold down the strings for lead playing. The thicker the gauge, the better the volume, the longer the sustain and the easier it is to keep the guitar in tune. A thicker gauge is also easier for rhythm playing. The common gauges are:

Ultra-light:	.008 (string 1) to .038 (string 6)
Extra-light:	.010 (string 1) to .050 (string 6)
Light:	.011 (string 1) to .052 (string 6)
Medium:	.013 (string 1) to .056 (string 6)
Heavy:	.014 (string 1) to .060 (string 6)

Strings come in three different main types: nylon, usually for Spanish or classical-style guitars; bronze, used for acoustic steel-strung instruments because they have little electrical quality; and steel strings, used for electric and acoustic instruments. You should never put steel or bronze strings on guitars that use nylon strings, as this will quickly ruin them.

With the exception of strings 1 and 2 (and sometimes 3), which are plain metal (as with bronze sets), steel strings are made up of a thread or core of wire around which another piece of wire is tightly wound. There are three types of winding:

- **Flatwound** – most commonly used on archtop guitars, a flat ribbon of steel is wound around a core of wire. Flatwound strings don't 'squeak' the way other strings can when you move your fingers along them, but they can produce a somewhat duller tone and are more likely to crack.
- **Roundwound** – most electric steel strings are roundwound, a piece of steel that is wound around a steel core. They have a brighter tone than flatwound, and often last longer, but seem a little harder to play at first.
- **Groundwound** – these are conventional roundwound strings that have been ground down to create a partially flat surface.

Changing Strings

Guitars are pretty rugged instruments, and changing strings regularly will improve the guitar's sound, help prevent strings breaking at the wrong moment, and help identify possible maintenance problems. (You may discover a rattling tuning peg, or a gouged bridge or nut.) Old strings tend to sound dull and lifeless, and become brittle with age. This makes them feel more difficult to fret and harder to keep in tune.

Removing the Old Strings

An old wives tale has it that replacing strings one at a time is better for the guitar because it maintains tension on the neck. Not true. Guitars are made of sterner stuff. However, replacing strings one at a time can be more convenient.

A potential problem with taking all the strings off at the same time is that on guitars with a movable bridge, the bridge *will* move. This isn't something you want to have happen, because repositioning a bridge can be a pain. And if the bridge is not positioned properly, it can affect the tuning of the strings and the feel of the neck as you play. A good compromise is to replace the strings three at a time. Replace the bass strings first, putting them in rough tune with the old treble strings, and then replace the treble strings, putting them in tune with the new bass strings. Then you can adjust the tuning of all six new strings.

It can be tedious to turn your tuning pegs. Save yourself time by buying a string winder, which fits over the tuning peg and allows you to turn it far more quickly.

You can just unwind the strings by lessening the tension using the tuning peg, or you can try a more radical approach and use wire cutters to snip the strings near the tuning peg. Once the old strings are off the guitar, throw them away.

Classical Guitars

Classical guitars have fixed bridges, so you can replace the strings all at once if you like. Nylon isn't as springy as steel, but attaching the string to the bridge can be tricky at first.

FIGURE 3(a):
Attaching nylon strings to a bridge

FIGURE 3(b):
Nylon strings attached to a bridge

FIGURE 4(a):
Attaching strings to a tuning peg

The arrow indicates the direction to turn the tuning peg.

FIGURE 4(b):
Order of strings as they are attached to the tuning pegs

Bass strings

Treble strings

Pass the string through the hole in the bridge, leaving about 38mm (1^1/$_2$in) sticking out at the back. Loop the short end back up, and wrap it behind the long end and then under itself. Pull it taut by tugging on the long end of the string. You may have to practise this a few times. Don't cut the string until everything is in place and in tune.

Thread the long end through the hole in the tuning peg at the head. (FIGURE 4(b) shows the order of the strings on the head.) Bring the end of the string over the roller (or capstan) in front of the hole and under itself. Make sure the string sits in the small groove on the nut. Then take up some of the slack of the string and tighten the tuning peg by winding the bass strings from right to left (anticlockwise), and treble strings from left to right (clockwise). As it picks up the slack of the string, the tuning peg will tighten and lock itself in place. While the string tightens, start tuning it and stretching it by pulling on it at various times. Once the guitar string is in place and in tune, snip away the excess string, leaving maybe 50mm (2in) at the tuning peg, and 25mm (1in) or less at the bridge.

Steel-Strung Acoustic Guitars

Archtop acoustic, a very few flat-top acoustic, and many electric guitars have a moveable bridge, so when you change the strings you want to be careful not to dislodge it. It's a good idea to change the strings one at a time, or three at a time, but not all at the same time, in order to keep the bridge anchored in its best position.

Most flat-top acoustic guitars have bridges that anchor the end of the string by popping the string into a hole and keeping it in place with a pin. First, loosen the string by slackening off the tension at the tuning peg. Then ease out the bridge pin.

Bridge pins can stick sometimes, so carefully use needle-nose pliers or the blunt edge of a table knife to ease the pin out of its hole. Be careful not to dig into the wood. Once the pin is out, you can remove the string.

Stuff the end of the new string that has a little brass ring into the bridge pin hole. Then wedge the bridge pin back into the hole, locking the ring and the string in place. You'll notice that the pin has a slot. Make sure this slot faces forwards (towards the tuning pegs).

Now pass the string over the bridge post, making sure each string fits snugly into the groove on the bridge and on the nut. Thread the loose end through the hole in the tuning peg post. If you want, you can put a small kink in the string to help keep it in place. Take up the slack on the string and then turn the tuning peg clockwise for the treble strings, and anticlockwise for the bass strings, tuning the string as the tension increases.

After all the strings are attached, retune the guitar carefully, bringing all the strings up to concert pitch. Be careful; you don't want to break a string. The best technique is to turn the tuning peg a couple of times, then check the tuning until you get the string in tune. When the string is in tune, clip the end off at the tuning peg, leaving about 25mm (1in) of extra wire protruding.

New strings need to be constantly checked, and then 'played in' before they settle into, and stay in, the correct tuning.

Electric Guitars

With most electric guitars, the string is attached to the bridge by passing one end through a hole in the back of the guitar and threading the string up to the brass ball, which keeps it in place. With a tailpiece, simply feed the loose string end through the appropriate hole and over the bridge.

Some guitars use what is called a locking nut system, such as a Floyd Rose tremolo unit. Here, the strings are clamped into place at the bridge saddle using a special Allen key. It's a good idea to use a piece of wood or a pack of playing cards to take up the tension when a string is changed; this stops the unit from rocking back and forth. On tremolo units, when one string is changed, the tension on all the strings changes.

In order to use these bridges, you must snip off the ball so that the string can be fitted into a small vice-like mechanism that holds the string in place. When all the strings are changed, you can remove the wood or playing cards supporting the bridge. Tune the strings as usual, using the tuning pegs. Then make the final adjustment on the bridge anchor using an Allen key. But be careful – don't overtighten the strings at the bridge too soon. If you do overtighten a string, when you remove the block supporting the unit, the string may snap as the tension increases.

Remember, if you have a guitar with this kind of bridge, the spare strings need to have the ball ends removed. Get into the habit of carrying wire cutters around in your guitar case.

Basic Repairs and Maintenance

The simplest thing to do to maintain your guitar is to clean it. If dust gathers under the head and bridge, clean them by using a cloth or feather duster, which can clean without the danger of scratching.

Natural oils from your fingers coat the strings every time you play. In time the strings start to corrode, and not only can this damage the strings' ability to sound good, it can eventually injure the wood of the instrument, seeping into the fingerboard. Wipe down the guitar after every playing session and before you put the guitar back in its case – front, sides, back, fingerboard and back of the neck. A chamois-leather cloth is a good investment because it not only cleans but polishes at the same time.

Use a cloth to clean each string. Hold the cloth between your thumb and index fingers, and then run it along the length of each string.

If the guitar has not been used for a while, first dust it and then rub down the wood with furniture polish or, better, guitar polish. (Some types of furniture polish contain abrasives that can damage the guitar's finish.) Never put polish directly onto the instrument, as it can damage the finish – put your cleaning solution onto a cloth first.

For the metal parts, you may want to use a mild jewellers' or chrome polish, so long as it's not abrasive.

Avoid keeping your guitar in a place that's subject to direct sunlight for long periods of time, or drastic changes in temperature and humidity. This will help keep the guitar surface from cracking. If you do accidentally chip the surface, take the guitar to a professional guitar repairer, who will easily fix the problem. If you decide to do it yourself, bear in mind that when you add or remove varnish, it can drastically change the wood's ability to vibrate, and thus the guitar's sound.

When travelling, keep the guitar inside the vehicle if you can. A guitar in the boot or luggage compartment can be subjected to extremes of heat and cold. If you have to put it in the boot, try to put it as close to the passenger compartment as possible, so if you're hit from behind, it stands a chance of surviving the accident.

Also, when travelling, carry your guitar in a hard case. If you're just going to a gig and back, a good padded nylon gig bag will offer some protection – but not much.

Be careful! Don't ever touch the pickups of an electric guitar with anything besides a dry brush or cloth. Pickups are electrical, and liquid can cause a short-circuit.

If your guitar has been subjected to extreme cold, when you bring it indoors, leave it in its case until it has had time to adjust to the room temperature. Remember, wood expands and contracts, and if it does so too rapidly, your instrument could get damaged. A good rule of thumb for storing your guitar: if you are comfortable with the temperature in the room, the guitar will be as well.

Alterations and Setting up the Guitar

Don't fiddle with these things until you're comfortable with the idea that you know what you're doing, and why you're doing it. In most cases, if you're consistently unhappy with how your instrument plays or sounds, you'll be better off taking your guitar to a professional repairer, who may even be able to fix these things while you wait. Professional repairers often spend time watching the musician play and talking about what the guitarist thinks is right or wrong about the instrument before deciding on the best way to set up the guitar.

Fret wire can wear out, and grooves will appear where the strings have worn away the nickel. Eventually the frets will start to buzz. Take your guitar to a professional repairer, who will replace the fret wire with the best gauge of fret wire for your guitar. Refretting can add a new lease of life to an old guitar.

Adjusting the Bridge

You can alter the action of your guitar by adjusting the bridge. The action describes the height of the strings above the fingerboard. The higher the action, the more strength you need to use to fret a note. It can be useful for rhythm playing, when you are principally playing chords all the time. Blues players who use slides often use a high action so the bottleneck or metal bar doesn't scrape against the frets.

The lower the action, the easier it is to fret the note. This can be useful for fast, single-note lead guitar playing.

Ideally, you want to set the action as low as you can without getting fret buzzing. This is really a trial-and-error process. (Bear in mind that the thickness of the gauge of string you use can make a difference to playability as well.) Before you make any adjustments to the action, make sure you are using a new set of strings. Old strings can affect the action and intonation.

On most electric guitars, each string has an adjustable saddle on the bridge. Either the saddle will have a screw that will adjust the whole bridge saddle at one go, or each string will have an individual screw that can be raised or lowered. Sometimes it's necessary to adjust the whole bridge saddle by filing it down. This should not be done by anyone except a professional repairer.

By changing the action, you are also affecting the intonation of the guitar. When you raise or lower the action, you alter the tension and distance between the bridge and the nut. This affects the way the strings play in tune. The distance between the nut and the 12th fret must be *identical* to the distance between the 12th fret and the bridge saddle. If it isn't, the guitar won't play in tune. The easiest way to test this is to play the string open, and then play the note at the 12th fret, or the harmonic at the 12th fret. It should be identical, though an octave higher. If the note at the 12th fret is sharp, the string is too short and must be lengthened by moving back the saddle. If the note is flat, move the saddle toward the nut.

Adjusting the Neck

Temperature changes, humidity and age can cause guitars to swell and contract. This in turn can affect the set-up of the guitar. For example, a slight bow in the neck can cause fret buzz, or difficulty getting a clean note at a particular fret or series of frets. You can sometimes adjust the neck by manipulating the truss rod, which runs down the centre of the neck just under the fingerboard. Not all guitars have truss rods, and some that do may not allow you to adjust them. (Rickenbackers and some other electric guitars have two truss rods, for separate back-and-forward and side-to-side adjustments.) Usually you can see whether the truss rod can be adjusted because there is a plate at the headstock near the nut. Once removed, you will see a rod with an adjustable screw or nut end. If you have a new guitar, it probably came with a truss rod Allen key or spanner.

If your guitar bows out between the seventh and 12th frets, you'll see a large gap between the strings and fretboard that makes playing the string at this point very hard. Tighten the truss rod, as you face it, by turning the nut a quarter-turn clockwise. Give the instrument a few moments after each turn to settle into its new position.

If the frets buzz and the neck bows inwards at the same place, you can loosen the truss rod by turning the nut a quarter-turn at a time anticlockwise (as you face the guitar). Again, allow the instrument to settle after each quarter-turn adjustment.

If you can't fix the problem within a few turns, stop and take the guitar to a professional repairer. Overtightening or overloosening the truss rod can ruin a guitar and make it permanently unplayable.

Loose Connections

If you hear a rattle, try strumming the instrument and touching various potential culprits with your free hand until you touch the correct object and the rattling stops. For example, it could be a loose screw in a tuning peg or a loose nut on a jack socket. It's a good idea to gather a small toolkit of screwdrivers, pliers, spanners and the like that fit the various sizes of screws and nuts on your guitar.

Tuning Pegs

Tuning pegs, tuning machines or machine heads (different names for the same thing) are easily replaced if gears get worn or a part breaks off. If more than one tuning peg is giving you trouble, it's probably a good idea to replace the whole set.

The tuning pegs screw into the wood of the head, so take off the string, unscrew the tuning peg, take the peg to a guitar store, and try to get a matching peg. Then screw the new peg into place in the same position as before. On Spanish, classical and some cheap flat-top acoustic guitars, the three pegs each side are mounted onto a single plate, and you may have to remove and replace the whole assembly.

Strap Pins

These are little buttons used to attach a strap to the guitar. They usually have regular screw bodies, and they can sometimes work themselves loose. If tightening the pin with a screwdriver doesn't work, dab a little plastic wood or PVA glue on the end and put it back. If you still have trouble, take the guitar to a professional.

Electrical Problems

Dust and other gunge can affect the electrics of your guitar. If your volume or tone controls start to crackle when you turn them, or you're getting a weak or inconsistent signal, you may have dust or something else on the control. Turn the knobs vigorously back and forth to see if you can work out the dirt. If that doesn't work, try spraying the controls inside with aimed blasts from a tin of compressed air or a tin of switch-cleaning fluid. If all else fails, go to a professional, who will give your controls a thorough cleaning.

The crackle can also indicate a loose wire in the jack plug. Take off the jack plate and look for the loose connection. If you spot it, use a soldering iron to reattach the wire to its appropriate lug. If you're uncomfortable doing this, take your guitar to a professional.

Replacing a pickup is not that difficult. Often the pickups that came with your guitar aren't as good as ones you could buy to replace them. Make sure you get a pickup that's the same size and type as the one you're replacing so it fits into the existing holes drilled into the body.

Make sure you know which wire is supposed to be soldered to which connection. Then seat the pickup in the cavity left by the old pickup, and screw it into place. Again, don't attempt this if you don't feel confident about being able to do the job.

CHAPTER 9

How to Get
a Good Sound

Sound is Personal

Once you reach a comfort level with strumming, playing chords and single-note playing, you should start to think about the kind of sound you want to get out of your instrument.

Sound is a mental thing. Two guitarists can sit down and use the same amp and guitar (and sometimes even the same acoustic instrument) and produce different sounds that identify the players, much as their voices identify them.

It's how you hear the sound that's important. Musicians of all instruments spend a lot of time experimenting and working on getting not just a good sound, but an individualistic sound. Who are your favourite players? Do you like their sound? Have you tried to re-create it? Investigated how they came up with their sound? In guitar magazines or interviews you can read how players used this guitar with that amp combined with that effect, but somehow when you try using the same set-up, it doesn't sound the same. The reason? The sound was in their head and was developed from listening to other guitarists or other instrumentalists they admired, together with years of experimentation.

Acoustic Guitars

For acoustic players, getting a good sound means fretting the note cleanly, so that it sounds loud and clear, and sustains well. (Saxophone players practise getting a good sound by playing one note and holding it for a long time, then moving to the next.)

The keys to a good sound are deliberateness – that is, you mean to sound the note and commit yourself to sounding it – and clean articulation. A great way to practise getting a clean sound is to play your scales very slowly and deliberately (there's that word again). Articulate each note of the scale as you fret it.

Electric Guitars

It's possible to play an electric guitar without an amplifier, but unless your guitar is a semi-acoustic or an archtop, the sound will be pretty dismal – rather like flies buzzing around your head, and about as loud.

After you've spent most (but not all, we hope) your money on your guitar, it's time to consider getting an amplifier. A good guitar and a decent amp go a long way to helping you create a good sound.

The History of Amplifiers

By 1930, anyone familiar with electricity knew that metal, moving through a magnetic field, caused a disturbance that could be translated into an electric current by a nearby coil of wire. Electrical generators and record player pickups already used this principle. The problem of building a guitar pickup was in creating a practical way of turning a string's vibration into a current.

After months of trial and error, Hawaiian steel-guitar player George Beauchamp – who, with Adolph Rickenbacker, formed the Electro String Company in the early 1930s – developed a pickup that consisted of two horseshoe magnets. The strings passed through these and over a coil, which had six pole pieces that concentrated the magnetic field under each string.

When the pickup seemed to work, Beauchamp enlisted Harry Watson, a skilled guitar maker for National Guitars, to make an electric Hawaiian guitar. It was nicknamed the 'Frying Pan'.

Electro String had to overcome several obstacles, however. To begin with, 1931 was the worst year of the Great Depression, and no one had money to spend on newfangled guitars. Further, only the most far-sighted of musicians saw the potential, and the Patent Office did not know if the Frying Pan was an electrical device or a musical instrument.

From the very beginning, Electro String developed and sold amplifiers – obvious, really, because without an amplifier the new electric guitar would have been useless. The first production-model amp was designed and built by a Mr Van Nest at his Los Angeles radio shop.

Soon after, Beauchamp and Rickenbacker hired design engineer Ralph Robertson to work on amplifiers. He developed the new circuitry for a line that by 1941 included at least four models. Early Rickenbacker amps influenced, among others, Leo Fender, who by the early 1940s was repairing them at his radio shop in nearby Fullerton, California.

By today's standards, the amps were pretty weak. Their output was about 10 watts, which is low, and they used radio technology, vacuum tubes and small loudspeakers. However, as the popularity of the electric guitar grew, there was a corresponding demand for louder amps.

The breach was filled by Leo Fender. In 1949 he worked with his engineer, Don Randall, to produce the first Super Amp model amplifier. With the Fender solid-bodied guitars (the Telecaster and Stratocaster) in general production, and the introduction of the Gibson Les Paul in 1952, the demand for amps went through the roof as the popularity of the solid body grew. Output rose to a reasonable 50 watts, with 12-inch speakers, still the norm for guitar amps (they are 305mm, but are always called '12-inch').

By the late 1950s, the British company Vox had produced the AC30, which is as much a classic amp today as the Fender Twin Reverb. The Vox was particularly popular with blues and rock musicians because it produced a warm tone, which musicians such as Jimi Hendrix, Jeff Beck and like-minded heavy-metal rockers discovered could be overdriven to create the fuzzy, distorted effect that has come to define the 1960s rock guitar sound.

Splitting up a combo amp into individual components came about during the rock era of the 1960s. The amp became known as the head, and the speakers became known as the stack. You could get more powerful amps and much bigger speakers this way, and by combining various amps and speaker combinations, musicians could produce more volume.

As the 1960s wore on, and rock bands played bigger and bigger venues, power and volume once more became a problem. This was solved when British engineer Jim Marshall produced a 100-watt amp connected to a stack of four 12-inch speakers. Pretty soon the Marshall stack was the norm for rock concerts.

By the 1970s, the vacuum-tube technology of the 1930s was finally being replaced by cheaper and more predictable solid state transistors, although musicians complained about the coldness of the sound, as compared to the warmth of the tube amp. It was popular among those who liked a thinner, cleaner sound.

The brittle sound was offset by the wider frequency range and the ability to play cleanly (without distorting) at higher volumes. Different tubes could produce different sounds, but needed to be replaced periodically because they came loose, or burned out.

By the 1980s, amplifier makers went back to creating a valve sound, often creating hybrid models that featured tube pre-amps and solid-state power amplifiers, getting the best of both worlds. Today, a traditional guitar amp combines an amplifier and a loudspeaker in one unit, called a combo. Most combos are compact and relatively easy to transport.

How Amps Work

Combo amps (and amps in general) come in a variety of sizes and shapes, but there are certain common functions that feature on most models. These are input sockets, individual channel volume controls, and tone controls, plus a master volume control.

There are two basic stages in producing a sound through a combo amp: the pre-amp, which controls the input volume and tone, and the power amp, which controls the overall volume. Most of the tone colours are created during the pre-amp stage.

The input socket takes the signal from the guitar, through the cable, or lead, which connects the guitar to the amp via a jack socket. If there is more than one input socket, other instruments, such as a second guitar, or a microphone, can be fed into the amp at the same time through these other input sockets.

Channel input volume controls allow the player to adjust the volume on the amp. They usually boost the signal from the guitar and pass that signal along to the tone controls.

Channel tone controls can often be as simple as bass and treble controls. More sophisticated models, such as the Mesa Boogie, feature a full-blown graphic equalizer. Basically, the controls split the sound into two or more bands, allowing for precise programming of the sound.

Output volume is the final stage of the process. The signal from the pre-amp passes through the power amplifier and is controlled by a master volume knob that controls the signal to the loudspeaker. The master volume controls the volume of the total output to the speaker, regardless of how many input channels are being used.

Other Controls

More sophisticated models have controls that affect distortion, reverb and tremolo. Speakers come in a wide range of sizes and can be linked together to produce different kinds and volume of sound. Basically, a loudspeaker is the opposite of a microphone. When a string creates a disturbance in the magnetic field around the pickup, the final adjusted signal (having passed through pre-amp and power amp) is passed to a voice coil, connected to a large diaphragm, often made out of cardboard or some other responsive and flexible material. The coil receives the signal, transmutes that into a magnetic field of its own, and causes the diaphragm and cone to vibrate. The vibration disturbs the surrounding air, and re-creates the sound waves that were originally generated by striking the guitar string.

Most guitar amp loudspeakers are rated by their impedance factor, which varies from 8 ohms to 16 ohms. (Impedance is an electrical term. Measured in ohms, it is the total opposition to the flow of the alternating current in a circuit, but don't worry if this makes no sense to you.) It's important that amp output and speaker impedance are matched up. Too high a rating and the overall volume of the combo will be reduced. Standard 12-inch speakers (although 10-inch and 15-inch are also common now) can be connected together in pairs or quads, although the way they are connected will affect the overall sound output.

Getting Started

It's a good idea to begin with a small practice amp that can deliver a good signal at 6 or 12 watts. In general, what you pay for in an amp is power, not features, so practice amps can be quite cheap – less than £70.

It's also worth bearing in mind that you can often plug your guitar into the auxiliary or tape jack of a home stereo unit. If the unit doesn't have a suitable jack plug socket, go to a local electronics shop and tell the salespeople what you want to do. They can usually find you an adapter plug that will allow you to plug the guitar jack into a phono plug that will work on the stereo unit.

Before you plug in, however, make sure the volume is right down on the stereo unit, or you'll risk blowing out the speakers. You can even connect small practice amps, with no speakers, to headphones. That way, you can get a range of effects – such as distortion, EQ and compression – without disturbing anyone else.

Effects

Electronic effects allow you to produce quite a range of tones and colours. Some new combo amps have effects built into them, but most of the time nearly all of the effects you want to produce will have to be created by interposing an effects unit of some sort between the guitar and the amp. The jack plug that would normally be inserted into the amp is inserted in the in socket of the effects unit, and another lead connects the out socket of the effects unit to the amp. Most effects units are powered by 9-volt batteries, although they also have a wall-socket transformer. A transformer that's not created for the unit can hum, damage the foot pedal, or not even work.

Reverb

This is a natural effect that gives the impression that the sound is bouncing off walls and ceilings. Modern units allow you to programme the parameters of the sound, such as the size and shape of the imaginary room. Reverb is often used to breathe life into dead sound, and is perhaps the most common effect used in a recording studio.

Delay

Like reverb, delay gives the sense of sound bounced off a faraway object. You can create different effects depending on the length of the delay, which is measured in milliseconds (500 milliseconds = half a second).

Echo

When the delay is long enough that the repeated signal can be heard as a distinct sound in its own right, then you have an echo. You can control the speed of the echo and get sounds that range from the early days of 1950s rock and roll to the experiments of Robert Fripp or Brian May of Queen.

Phase and Flange

Phasing takes place when the same signal sounds as though it is being played back from two different sources at the same time. When the two signals are slightly out of sync – that is, when the peaks of the soundwave of one signal are overlaid on the valleys of the second signal – you get a sweeping sound called phase cancellation, which sounds a little like a revolving Leslie speaker for a Hammond organ, popular in the 1970s. If the delay is more dramatic, then the sweeping sound becomes known as flanging.

Chorus

By adding variations in pitch to a delayed signal, it's possible to create the sound of a doubled signal, as if a six-string guitar has become a 12-string, in a simple analogy (but without the extra octaves a 12-string provides).

Pitch Shifting

Here, the signal is digitally sampled – a 'piece' of a recorded track is digitally copied and then fed into a loop to be played endlessly. Then it is replayed at a different speed, which changes the original pitch to a new pitch. Units often have a range of an octave above and an octave below the original note. If, for example, you set the unit to play sixths, then every sound that goes into the unit will be played a major sixth higher.

Distortion

The most well-known of all effects, distorted sound can be created in a number of different ways. The volume of the signal is boosted to the point of distortion in a pre-amp, and then that distorted signal is amplified by the power amp.

Compression

Often used in conjunction with other effects, compression makes guitar notes sustain for a longer period, giving them more body, although it smoothes out the overall dynamics of a note.

Wah-Wah

Wah-wah is a sound from the 1960s and 1970s, popularized by Frank Zappa and Jimi Hendrix. A foot pedal controls a filter similar to a guitar's tone control, causing an almost vocal-like quality on occasion. The rhythm guitar sound in the original soundtrack of the film *Shaft*, for instance, is a typical wah-wah funk sound.

Tremolo

This is an effect that has a dated 1950s retro sound. Solid-body guitars used to have tremolo arms that could be manually activated. Now tremolo primarily comes in a pedal unit, and it sounds as though you're playing through a slowly moving fan. However, tremolo arms are standard equipment on Fender Stratocasters even today.

Volume Pedal

This is a pedal that can be set so that you can alternate between playing lead guitar and rhythm guitar at the dip of a switch. The pedal instantly raises or lowers the volume of the amplifier.

Combining Effects

Effects pedals can be combined, linking them together. However, the exact sequence of effects used can change the sound, depending on whether a particular effect is placed before or after another. If you use more than one effect, it's probably worthwhile considering buying a switching foot pedal unit that will help you control which effect you want to dominate your sound, and in what order you want the effects to be.

A modern solution to this problem has been the development of multiple-effects pedals, which can be programmed to remember a particular sound, or sequence of sounds, and also does away with a suitcase full of effects pedals littering the floor. Modern multi-effects, including the Pod series, allow you to create specific sounds, such as 'Fender Strat'.

Effects will not make you play better, or help you disguise mistakes. If you can't play well acoustically, you won't play better with a bunch of tricks loaded onto your guitar.

Choose your effects with care. They can date you, and they can interfere with the tracking of the guitar signal, making it seem as though you are constantly playing out of sequence with the other members of the group. Always carry a good supply of batteries if you don't have a transformer, and practise with the effect at home before you use it on a gig or for recording.

Tips for Buying an Amp

- Think about what you want the amp for. You're paying for power, mostly, so do you really need that 100-watt monster? Could you get way with a 50-watt combo instead? Or maybe even a practice amp until you start gigging?
- Size is important. Imagine yourself lugging your guitar and amp from gig to gig, going up and down narrow staircases, onto high stages... get the picture?
- Have you played your guitar through it? Never buy an amp without trying your guitar through it first to make sure it will do what you want it to do.
- Brand new or used? If used, then make sure the amp hasn't been so badly treated that it has had the guts ripped out of it.
- When the amp is switched on, listen. What for? Ideally, silence. Are there hums, buzzes, hisses? If so, beware.
- Check the speaker cone to make sure it's in one piece and not ripped or dented, or otherwise damaged.
- Test all the electrics, including switches and knobs, to make sure they work.
- Try out a variety of amps before you settle on the one you want to live with for a while.
- A tube amp will be heavier, but it will give you a warmer sound. A transistor amp will be easier to fix, and will be more flexible if you want to use a variety of sounds with your guitar.

CHAPTER 10

How to Record Yourself

A Brief History

From about the turn of the 20th century, the only way to capture sound was by first cutting a cylinder or a disc. Fairly quickly, the disc became the preferred method. In a recording studio, a wax disc was placed on a platter, and a needle attached to a microphone was placed at the outer edge of the disc. As the musician or group performed, the needle cut a continuous groove that recorded the sound.

When a vinyl impression of the master wax disc was made, to play the recording you essentially reversed the procedure. A needle was attached to a speaker, and when it was placed in the groove of the record and played at 78 revolutions per minute (rpm), you got a pretty accurate re-creation of the original recording session.

It was a bare bones, one-take deal, however. No re-recording, no repairing errors, no using the disc again. Furthermore, it all had to be done within three or four minutes, the length of time it took to go from the outside to the inside of the wax disc. Considering the demands of recording these discs, the performances that were captured are even more amazing when compared to what can be done today in the studio.

From the 1930s, tape recorders began to become available. These worked on the same principles as today: spools of tape coated with a magnetic oxide passed over a series of record and playback heads (or readers) on a tape machine. The big advantages of tape included the ability to edit the tape (using a razor blade and special glue or adhesive tape), the ability to re-record or reuse the tape, and the ability to record longer pieces of music at one time. However, one drawback was that you couldn't make too many copies tape-to-tape because the quality of the recording would degenerate.

Multitrack recorders came into use in the 1940s, allowing for the recording of a rhythm track on one channel and for other tracks to be overdubbed on other channels. The subsequent recordings were then balanced, mixed and mastered onto a separate tape recorder. Up to the 1950s, everything had been monaural or mono, the musical equivalent of black and white. Everything could be heard through one speaker. However, with the introduction of stereo, it was as though sound took on the musical equivalent of Technicolor. The invention of speakers with their own amplifiers meant that it was possible for each speaker to contain elements of the whole recording, creating the illusion that the drums were in the right speaker, the double bass in the left speaker, and the solo instrumentalist in the middle of the room, between the two speakers.

The psychedelic 1960s developed the stereo concept in wild and woolly ways as multitrack recorders went from four tracks to 16. By the 1970s, this number had increased to 24 individual tracks.

In fact, during the 1970s, the development of quadraphonic sound meant that the listener could be placed in the middle of a room surrounded by four speakers. Somehow, it never caught on as it should have, although it forms the basis of what is now known as 'surround sound' for home-entertainment systems.

The most radical of the digital inventions of the late 1980s and beyond was the invention of a computer protocol known as MIDI, which stands for Musical Instrument Digital Interface. This system of coding allows computers, synthesizers, drum machines and digital effects units to talk to each other. It has revolutionized home recording, allowing garage musicians the ability to produce professional-quality recordings quickly and inexpensively. Paradoxically, the development of music genres that use digital sampling, such as hip-hop, means that you can be proficient in manipulating MIDI machines to create music without necessarily being proficient as a musician to create sounds.

The 1990s saw the greatest revolution in recording since the introduction of the tape recorder – digital technology. Digital audio tape (DAT) recorders replaced larger analog reel-to-reel machines, and the quality of recording became much cleaner. Background tape hiss was eliminated, and the final recording could be copied as many times as needed without the signal being degraded each time.

You can now buy software for Apple Macs and PCs that allows you to manipulate high-quality, multitrack digital recordings that can be edited on-screen at the soundwave level. With the introduction of rewritable CDs and DVDs, and the increasing popularity of Sony Minidisk recorders and MP3 recorders, we are entering a brave new world of audio manipulation. It's perhaps worth reminding ourselves that the best recordings are about how the performer conveys emotion to the audience, and that the palette of emotions we should draw upon is often much broader than many musicians currently explore.

A word of warning: recording is a vast and complicated field. This chapter can only introduce you to some of the concepts, and offer a few words of advice.

Engineers, Tape Ops and Producers

In a small studio, many jobs are done by the engineer and/or the producer. However, in a larger studio, the engineer is responsible for recording all the performers and getting the final version down on tape, CD or DVD. The average engineer knows which microphone is best for which instrument and which singer, and also has an intimate knowledge of the different kinds of recording equipment used to capture and manipulate the sound of the session. Many modern engineers are tonmeisters – engineers with a university or college degree in recording engineering.

Tape ops are often trainee engineers. They basically serve as the studio gofers, doing everything the engineer and musicians don't want to do. Some of the world's best-known engineers and producers started life as tape ops.

Producers are a wide array of people. Their principle role is to be an objective pair of ears for the performer, helping him or her achieve the sound they want. One example of a great producer is George Martin, a classically trained musician who produced the Beatles by understanding and translating the ideas of Lennon and McCartney. Some have called him the 'fifth Beatle'. Another great producer is the brilliant jazz trumpeter and arranger Quincy Jones.

There are those who call themselves producers whose main expertise is sampling. They take a vocal track and build up layers of sound around the vocal, as in hip-hop recordings.

Do you need a producer for your recording? Only in the sense that you need someone who can objectively keep you on track and help you achieve your vision of what you want to create. Of course, this presumes you have a vision before you go into the studio. If you don't, the recording experience may end up being long, exhausting and expensive – and the end result probably not very good.

Recording Studio Basics

Studio performing is very different from live gigs. The studio can be a cold and impersonal place, and the studio experience can be detrimental to the creative experience.

You have several options when it comes to recording:

· You can try to capture a live gig.
· You can go into a professional studio.
· You can try to create a professional demo using home equipment.

A professional studio will have pretty much all the hardware and software you'll need for your recording, but it will also cost you money. A 24-track recording involving lots of overdubs and edits can be both time-consuming and expensive.

Depending on your budget, you may want to consider a direct live recording, with no overdubs. This may take as much as a couple of hours to set up for sound, and then an hour per track to record. Alternatively, you may want to select a more adventurous multitrack recording. Here, the rhythm section (drums, bass, rhythm guitar and/or piano) are recorded playing together. The lead guitar and vocal tracks are then overlaid afterwards. In general, the more tracks you overdub, the longer it takes to record and mix each track. It's possible you can spend all day (or longer) recording just one track this way, so be prepared. Either way, you will have to choose between the number of tracks you want to lay down, and what you can afford to pay for.

Make sure you shop around before making a final decision on a recording studio. Don't allow your excitement to cloud your judgment.

Recording Studio Tips

- If you decide to use a studio, ask around and try to find musicians who have recorded there. See if they recommend the studio, and find out why. Try not to rely on just one person's opinion, however. When you visit the studio, ask to hear samples of what they've done, and check out the condition of the equipment. Worn or poor equipment may interfere with your recording and add to your time in the studio – and you will be paying for the studio on an hourly basis.
- Make sure the recording engineer and the producer are familiar and comfortable with the kind of music you want to record.
- Make sure you know exactly what you are going to get for your money. For example, does the studio fee include the final mix? Copies of the final mix? Studio-owned instruments you can use? What are the other expenses?
- Unless money is no object, only record material that you have rehearsed and know well. A studio is a daunting place, and not conducive to jamming unless you're experienced.
- Make sure your equipment (strings, leads, amp and so forth) is in good condition before you bring it into the studio.
- Be on time, particularly if it's not your gig and someone else is paying for the studio time.
- Rather than trying for ten hastily recorded tracks, opt for four or five well-recorded ones.
- Make use of what's at hand, particularly other musicians. Lay down all the rhythm tracks, for example, and then come back if necessary to overdub the lead and vocal tracks.
- Keep the session a 'closed set', and don't make it a party. Have fun, but don't be distracted by having friends and acquaintances hanging out, getting in the way and trying to act as 'co-producer'.
- If you're unhappy with something, re-record it. Don't be easily satisfied with the old saw, 'We can fix it in the mix'. Trust us, you'll hear that clunking note until the day you die if you don't! Don't be too much of a perfectionist, however – you have to strike a balance.
- Make sure you have some kind of final-mix policy before you start the session. All the musicians involved will be focused on their

performance alone, and someone is going to have to be in charge of the final mixdown. If it's your record, it shouldn't be a problem. If you're a sidesman (or woman), you may have to deal with – and accept – someone else's opinion on what the overall sound will be like, and your place in it.

· Do the final mix a week or more after the initial recording, so that you can come back to the session with fresh ears.

Ten Commandments for the Studio

1. *If it ain't broke, don't fix it.* Whether you record on your Fostex at home or 48-track digital in a world-class studio, remember Duke Ellington's maxim: If It Sounds Good, It Is Good. If you like the sound you're getting, (a) don't change it, and (b) if you have to change it, remember what made it sound good in the first place.

2. *If it's broke, fix it.* The corollary to Number 1 is that if it sounds awful on tape, you won't be able to 'fix it in the mix'. If a track is not cutting it, change it or drop it. Try equalizing, compressing and editing (if it doesn't take too much time at the end of the session), or adding another microphone. The key is to be honest with yourself. If necessary, admit that (a) your favourite overdub isn't working; (b) the musical idea isn't cutting it; (c) the vocalist or instrumentalist is 'off' today; or (d) the performer just can't cut it. One way or another, move on.

3. *Keep it simple.* Mixing is like cooking: too many spices can ruin the dish. Move faders sparingly, 1 dB at a time. The mix always sounds great at 10 on the big speakers. The trick is to make it sound great at 3 on little speakers.

4. *Happy people make good music.* If something personal is worrying you, leave it at home. If something in the studio annoys you, try not to ruin a good mood. It can stop a session dead. Good music comes when musicians and technicians alike are having fun.

5. *Be prepared.* Be rehearsed and bring everything you need. Losing an hour of studio time because you don't have a spare set of strings or a 9-volt battery is infuriating and costly, and drives everyone in the

studio crazy. Be early! The clock starts at the appointed hour, not when you get there, and there's never enough time.

6. *Speaking of time...* If you have tempo troubles, rehearse the track slower. If anything sounds out of tune, check it. Use an empty track to record and try to mix great performances with minor time or intonation problems. If you were inspired, you may never quite get that feeling again.

7. *Respect studio staff.* Try not to be a pain for the studio staff, but remember, if you're paying, they're working for you. If the engineer says that something sounds great and you disagree, don't let it pass. Just pick your battles. If the vocal sounds awful, insist that it's done the way you want it. If that overdub stinks, mute it in the mix.

8. *Know what to record.* No amount of technical magic can compensate for mediocrity. When you gig, the audience tells you what they like. Nine times out of ten, the songs that come alive are the ones the public like best. Determine your list of tunes in advance based on the feedback you've received.

9. *Beat the pre-demo blues.* Don't put endless hours into a home demo and then go into a real studio to try to re-create it. Instead, try to channel your energy into the studio recording session.

10. *Know when to go home.* When your fingers get sore and your ears get tired, even if you have more time booked, go home and come back another day when you're fresher. Slow time in the studio comes in the beginning, as you are trying to get the right sound. Wasted time comes at the end. Remember what is important: (a) rhythm tracks; (b) vocals; (c) solos; (d) overdubs; and (e) effects.

Creating a Home Studio

When you're planning to create a home set-up, you need to consider how much money and space you can devote to the studio. A dedicated garage space or basement with a permanent studio set-up will give you a distinctly different sound and set-up to a few mikes, a Fostex DAT recorder, and a MIDI-ready Apple Mac in your front room.

The science of acoustics is too involved to get into here, but an empty room may sound very 'live' (clap your hands in such a room, and listen to the echo); the same room with curtains, carpeting and furniture will sound much 'deader'. Consider what you are going to record, and how best to record it. Drums, for example, may need to be in a deader space than vocals, which may need a more live environment.

Before jumping into the commitment of a home studio, carefully consider the cost and time involved. To get the best results, you need to be dedicated to the outcome of the project.

Are you going to use an old-fashioned analog four-track reel-to-reel recorder, such as Teac's Portastudio or the Fostex X series of cassette tape recorders, or a more modern digital system? Most people go for the digital system these days, but money will dictate what you can afford. Perhaps you'll be able to pick up some decent secondhand equipment on eBay, or at a local shop.

Digital systems come in two basic versions:

1. Real-time tape machines
2. Computer-based, hard-disk recording systems.

Real-Time Recorders

One of the most popular systems is the ADAT system, developed by Alesis and also used by Fostex. Eight tracks can be recorded individually or together on super VHS videotape. Through the magic of MIDI, digital recording allows a series of machines to be linked together as 'slave' machines that can be controlled by a 'master' machine if needed.

Hard-Disk Systems

The most common hard-disk systems are computer-based. For years Apple Mac reigned supreme, but these days there are similar systems for PCs. One advantage of a hard-disk system is that the recording can be easily edited at an almost 'atomic' note-by-note level. Another bonus is that you can cut and paste whole sections as easily as if you were using a word processor. Recordings can also be sequencer-based, which means that digital sounds can be mixed with MIDI tracks.

Home Recording Systems

Apple Macintosh

A lot of recording studios use Apple Mac computers for their DAT installations. If you decide to use a Mac, you'll need the following:

- A PCI-bus Power Mac, especially if the computer has PCI expansion slots and 16-bit audio capabilities. If you buy a used machine, try to find a machine that can be upgraded to a G3, G4 or G5 processor. Get as much RAM installed as you can afford. The absolute minimum you should have is 64MB, although 128MB or more will make things run much more smoothly. The eMac and G6 are the newest Mac computers. They come fitted with an IDE hard drive, a CD-ROM drive, and decent quality 16-bit audio built in, and USB and FireWire (IEEE1394) ports, which means you'll have to buy brand-new USB MIDI interfaces, or get a USB-to-serial adapter and install USB and MIDI driver updates.
- A big SCSI or FireWire hard drive (at least 40GB is best). The FireWire interface is probably the interface of the future. It can be used for hard drives and should be usable with CD-recordable drives, too. FireWire allows for hot-swappable connection of up to 64 devices, and allows for a theoretical maximum throughput of around 40MB/second. There is no such thing as a 'Mac-only' SCSI or FireWire hard drive. SCSI is SCSI and FireWire is FireWire, whether in a Mac or a PC, which does simplify matters a bit.

Software is generally more expensive for a Mac, but some of it is pretty good, such as Mark of the Unicorn Digital Performer, TC/Works Spark XL, and Bias Peak. There is also some Mac music shareware around, though nothing like what is available for a PC.

Windows-Based PCs

Once upon a time, the Windows-based PC platform was no match for Macintosh in the artistic arenas of sight and sound. That is no longer true. If you're willing to become a bit of a computer nerd, you can get a lot of power for less money than buying a Mac.

Hardware

Pentium III or better, AMD, or Celeron chip processors are the most widely compatible with all the various soundcards and other peripherals for use with PCs. Using anything slower than a Pentium 166 will make it very hard to work on stereo digital audio files for CD mastering. Stick to well-known name brands, and you should be OK. However, pay attention to compatibility issues between peripherals. If you're really set on a particular soundcard or audio interface, check on the manufacturer's website for links to user forums or newsgroups, where you can read about users' experiences with various types of peripherals and software. You may find that advanced features of a particular soundcard won't work in your favourite audio program, or that a certain video card will cause problems in your particular system.

For the operating system, most people will run either Microsoft Windows 98 SE, Windows ME, Windows 2000, Windows NT 4.0 or Windows XP. If you intend to use USB or FireWire devices, you'll be better off using Windows 98, Windows 2000 or Windows XP.

If you are doing extensive MIDI work, you'll need good MIDI timing and lots of MIDI channels. By turning off the extra bells and whistles that Windows 98 installs by default (look at the Tweak UI program on the installation disk under tools/reskit/powertools), you can usually get very good MIDI timing in your sequencer applications. Also, check out 98 Lite (www.98lite.com) for tips on how to strip Windows 98 down to its bare essentials.

A word of caution: software that requires Microsoft DirectX 5.0 or later will probably not work under Windows NT. This includes software synths like GigaSampler, Seer Systems Reality, FruityLoops or Roland Virtual Sound Canvas. There is an unofficial, unsupported patch that installs DirectX 5.0 in NT, but there are absolutely no guarantees with these kinds of hacks. Search on the Internet for a file named NT4DX5.zip, but use your own judgment.

Linux is fast becoming a viable OS alternative, and there is a lot of work going on aimed at making Linux a workable OS for the masses. A few soundcards are currently supported in Linux, including the Sonorus STUDI/O, SEK'D Prodif Gold, Zefiro Acoustics ZA-2, Aureal Vortex 2 (Turtle Beach Montego II and Diamond MX-300) and the Ensoniq AudioPCI (audio only), while the venerable Roland MPU-401 is supported for MIDI I/O.

Anyone interested in exploring Linux should check out the website www.4front-tech.com and http://sound.condorow.net, the Linux MIDI and Sound Application website.

PCs don't always come with built-in sound, so you may have to buy and install your own soundcard. It pays to do your homework before you buy a card. You will want either a big IDE or SCSI hard drive (at least 40GB or more). A SCSI drive will give you better performance.

Software

There is a lot of high-quality Windows music shareware available on the Internet. Don't be afraid to try these programs out; some are excellent. Two great shareware stereo sound editors are Cool Edit 2000 and GoldWave. Of course, there are tremendous commercial Windows sound editors, such as Sound Forge, Cool Edit Pro, Samplitude, Steinberg WaveLab and SAW, as well as MIDI/Audio sequencers such as Cakewalk Pro Audio, Steinberg Cubase VST and Emagic Logic Audio on the high end, with PG Music Power Tracks Pro Audio and FASoft-n-Track.

 Can't decide which system to use? Remember that the more complex the system you choose, the more time you will have to spend learning how to use and manipulate the result, and the less time playing music.

There are a number of things that can mess up a PC's ability to play and record clean-sounding digital audio – resource-greedy device drivers, overintrusive antivirus programs and fancy fax software come to mind immediately. If your first priority is music, make sure you fine-tune your system for that, rather than, for example, playing games.

CHAPTER 11

How to Practise

Good Habits

The key to good practice habits is consistency. Ten minutes a day – every day – is better than eight hours once a week on a Saturday afternoon. Your fingers have to learn a 'muscle memory' of how to form the chords and where to go and what to do, and you have to get over the slight soreness of your fingertips until the calluses build up. (A hint: if your fingertips get sore, take a break and dip them in some surgical spirit.)

Knowing how to practise, and what to practise, can mean the difference between spending hours spinning your wheels in one place, and advancing by leaps and bounds with only an hour or two a day.

First Things First

The first thing you should try to get is a professional teacher, a decent instrument and a good method book. (You can find a list of some useful books in the Appendix.)

You have to be honest with yourself about how much time you can put into practising. Ideally, your practice time and place should be the same every day. You should practise in a well-lit area with a comfortable chair and a music stand.

Write out a schedule for yourself and stick to it. It is absolutely imperative that you practise in a relaxed manner. If you strain, you'll run the risk of muscle problems with your shoulders or your hands. Take lots of breaks during your practice session, partly to relax and help the muscles, and partly to ensure that you don't build in mistakes into your playing technique in an attempt to get to the next stage as quickly as possible.

If your hands start to tighten up or get cramp, stop and take deep breaths, which will ease the tension and calm you down at the same time. Take walks. Remember that – paradoxically – you will improve much faster if you allow your hands and fingers to develop slowly and at their own speed.

A Practice Schedule

It would be great if you could practise for two hours every day, but few of us can. Practising is a highly personal thing, and what works for one person doesn't always work for someone else. That said, there *are* certain things you should try to do.

Be consistent. Try to spend five or ten minutes every day on the same thing. Repetition breeds a familiarity that creates a confidence that will help you on to the next stage. This can become tedious and boring, however, so you have to strike a balance between maintaining your interest and perfecting your skills.

If you can't do something every day, try to do it two or three times a week. Again, the keys are repetition and consistency. Spread the work over several days. Be sure you do this every week consistently.

For example:

Monday: Do some method book exercises and major scales.

Tuesday: Do some picking and strumming exercises, open-string chords and minor scales.

Wednesday: Work on more method book items and sharpen your music-reading skills.

Thursday: Learn some harmony and work on more songs.

Friday: Start the sequence all over again.

Remember, take lots of breaks and stay relaxed. If something is hard, try it a couple of times and then go on to something else. In a while, return to the hard exercise and chip away at it bit by bit.

Beginner's Practice Schedule (two hours)

20 minutes: work through four pages of method book

20 minutes: practise major scales (open position)

20 minutes: spend time learning major, minor and 7th open-string chords

20 minutes: alternate right-hand picking exercises

20 minutes: study music theory and harmony

10 minutes: practise barre chords

10 minutes: strum chords to some simple songs from the method book

You should try to stick to this for seven to ten days, although there is no real time limit; everyone learns at a different rate. When you're comfortable, you can change it around a little.

These principles of practice are really the same whatever level of playing you've reached. The only difference is the kinds of thing you'll be practising.

Intermediate Player's Practice Schedule (two hours)

20 minutes: work through six to eight pages of intermediate method book

20 minutes: practise major and minor scales (up to 5th position)

20 minutes: practise chords

20 minutes: work on right-hand alternate consecutive picking exercises

20 minutes: learn to read music in different positions

10 minutes: work on triad and 7th chord arpeggios

10 minutes: learn chords and melodies to more advanced songs, such as 'Blackbird', 'Over the Rainbow', 'Satin Doll' etc.

The intermediate schedule may look daunting now, but by the time you reach that level, it will make pretty good sense.

LESSON 1

Holding the Guitar and Writing Music

Sitting

Before you start playing, you need to be able to cradle the guitar comfortably so that you're relaxed when you play. There are a number of way of doing this. Let's begin with sitting.

The traditional, classical guitar position is to raise the neck of the guitar to about 45 degrees from the vertical – that is, you want the head of the instrument about level with your shoulder, while the 'waist' of the guitar rests on your left thigh. Place your left foot on an adjustable footstool to help create this effect. By holding the neck at this angle, you get the maximum positioning of your left hand on the fretboard and your right hand over the strings. The hands do not support the neck in this position.

FIGURE 1-1:
Classical pose

FIGURE 1-2:
Informal
seated pose

The more informal seated position is to rest the waist of the guitar on your right thigh, while the inside of your right arm holds the body of the instrument in place, and your left hand gives slight support to the neck.

If you have a solid-bodied electric guitar, the seated position can be awkward because the weight of the head and neck will dip down, making the guitar hard to play. You need to use a shoulder strap.

Standing

If you decide to play standing up, make sure you buy a good strap that will comfortably support the weight of the guitar and not cut into your shoulder at the same time.

FIGURE 1-3:
Standing pose

The guitar should hang comfortably against your body, leaving both your arms free. If the strap is adjusted properly, the neck of the guitar should be at about a 45-degree angle. The bridge should be about level with your waist, and the head about level with your shoulder.

We know, you saw some rock idol playing with the guitar at his ankle level, and it looked really cool. After you know what you're doing, you can adjust the instrument any way you want. But for now, as a beginner, don't make life harder for yourself than it has to be. Playing with the guitar slung too low can really strain your hands and wrists.

Left-Hand Position

To begin with, the best way to fret a note cleanly is to exert the maximum pressure using your fingertips. The key is to develop a good left-hand technique. First, let the edge of the neck of the guitar rest in the palm of your left hand. You'll notice that your thumb and fingers automatically fall to either side of the neck. Now place the left-hand thumb in the middle of the back of the neck so that there is space between the neck and your palm. You should be able to pivot your whole hand on the ball of your thumb without banging into the neck.

FIGURE 1-4:
Placing the thumb
in the middle of the
back of the neck

FIGURE 1-5:
Holding the string
against the fret with
the fingertip pad
(Note: each finger
to a fret)

When you fret a note, use the tip or pad of your finger to press the note firmly to the fingerboard. If you put your thumb immediately behind the place where you're pressing the string to the fretboard (as if you're trying to pinch thumb and finger together through the neck), you'll get maximum pressure on the note and it will sound clean.

FIGURE 1-6:
FIGURE 1-7:
Left-hand
positions

In classical guitar parlance, they talk about the right and left hands looking like two swans' necks. That may be a bit much for most players, but try the following exercise. Place the tip of your first finger on the first string at the first fret. (Look at FIGURE 1-8.) Now pluck the string with your right-hand thumb by the soundhole.

In FIGURE 1-9, each vertical line represents a string. Each horizontal line represents a fret wire. The double line at the top represents the guitar nut. The black dot or number represents the finger you should use to stop that string at that fret – in this case, at the note F on the first string.

Press the string to the fretboard roughly in the middle of the fret (between the fret wires). If you press too close to a fret wire, the string may be muted; too far away and the string may buzz. To make sure you don't mute other strings, make a point of using your fingertips and keeping your fingers as vertical as possible to the strings by arching your wrist slightly (like a swan's neck). The classical guitar technique helps in this regard.

A lot of players let their left-hand thumb come over the top of the neck. They even use it to fret bass notes. This is perfectly fine, but it's hard for beginners to do. Remember, the more your hand is cramped, the harder it is to play the note well (that is, without any buzzing sound), and the more your muscles may ache.

FIGURE I-8:
FIGURE I-9:

As soon as your hand or fingers get sore or start to hurt, stop! It will take a little time for the strength in your fingers to build up. Playing a little bit often is better than playing a lot in one go.

Right-Hand Position

The right hand can be used fingerstyle, which means that each finger of the right hand manipulates the strings (as in classical or folk/blues finger-picking styles). Alternatively, you can hold a plectrum or pick in your right hand to strum rhythms or pick out notes on the strings.

Fingerstyle

The basic fingerstyle position is to use the fingernails to pluck the strings. (Initially, you may use your fingertips as well.) The fingers are held vertical to the strings with a slight arch in the wrist. (Remember the idea of a swan's neck?) The thumb plays the three bass strings, while the first finger plucks the third string, the second finger the second string, and the third finger the first string. (The little finger is not often used.)

FIGURE 1-10:
Right-hand
position

For the moment, it's probably a good idea to practise strumming all six strings first with a pick, and then using just your thumb. The key is to place your fingertips on the fingerplate to anchor your hand, and then brush your thumb across all the strings. We'll discuss more complex fingerpicking and pick techniques further on.

Holding a Pick

The size and thickness of a pick (also known as a plectrum) can vary greatly. In the beginning, you need one that has a medium size and thickness. Buy yourself two or three, and experiment.

Let the pick lie flat on your first finger, and then comfortably hold it in place with your thumb. You can then use it to strum the string with up-and-down motions. The movement comes from the wrist, not the fingers.

FIGURE 1-11:
Holding a pick

FIGURE 1-12:
Using the pick
to strum

To get a feel of what to do, take your right hand and extend the fingers, with the thumb and first finger lightly touching at the tip. With the fingertips still touching, shake your hand up and down at the wrist in a gentle motion. This is the motion you want to use to strum the guitar strings.

Getting it Down on Paper

There are three basic ways to write down music for the guitar.

Chords and Slashes

The first way uses chord symbols and slashes, which represent the number of times you should strum a chord. Each slash represents one down stroke or strum of a chord.

FIGURE 1-13:
Written music
using chord
symbols and
slashes

Chords are also written down in boxes, which are really representations of the fingerboard. Each vertical line is a string, and each horizontal line is a fret wire.

FIGURE 1-14:
E (major)

Fret 1

(numbers are fingers to use
on your left hand)

E

Each circle or number represents a place where you should put your finger on the fretboard and the finger you should use to stop the note. The name of the chord is written under the diagram.

If you look at the chord diagram in FIGURE 1-14, you'll see that the chord has a distinctive 'shape'. Let's call this one the E shape. Each finger has a certain place it should be on the fingerboard in order to play the E chord. If you move your fingers across one string towards the treble end (i.e. the chord shape starts not on string 5 but on string 4), the E shape will make the chord A minor. (Don't worry about why for now.) It's a good idea to think about chords as shapes that can be moved around the fingerboard. It will come in very useful later on.

The right-hand fingers are numbered as shown in FIGURE 1-15.

FIGURE 1-15:
The hand,
numbered

Guitar Tablature

Another way to write down music is using guitar tablature.

FIGURE 1-16:
Guitar tablature

strings   fret number   open string   bar line   E Maj chords

Here, each line represents a string on the guitar, with the top line the first string, and the bottom line the sixth string. The numbers on each line represent the fret you need to stop in order to get a note. You can show complex fingerings this way, including chords and melodies. This system is used by many guitarists.

Standard Notation

Finally, there is standard notation. This looks a lot like tablature, except that instead of six lines, there are only five.

FIGURE 1-17:
Standard notation

We will get into how to read music later on. It's enough to know that you can do a lot more with standard notation than with almost any other system of musical notation, and learning to read music isn't that hard. Music only has seven main letters – C, D, E, F, G, A and B – and then it starts all over again. With a little regular practice, you'll be reading music in no time.

LESSON 2

First Songs
and Chords

Chords C and G7

Now you're going to learn to strum some songs. To do this, you need a few chords. A chord is made when three or more strings are played together, by strumming with a pick or plectrum, or using your thumb.

The chords we are going to show you now are easy versions of fuller open string chords you'll learn later. Their names are C and G7. Try to memorize the names of the chords and the shapes they make. Note that 'O' above a string means that it is played open (not fretted).

FIGURE 2-1(a):
C

C

FIGURE 2-1(b):
G7

G7

To play the chord C major, put your first finger on the second string at the first fret. Press hard. Strum Strings 1, 2, and 3 together four times. You've now strummed four beats. When it is written this way, it is a bar of music: | C / / / |

Strum the chord four more times. You've now strummed two bars of C: (| C / / / | C / / / |)

To play the chord G7, put your first finger on the first string at the first fret. Play the first three strings again, strumming four times.

Play the C chord four more times. And then another four times. Play G7 four times. Now play C four times.

Surprise! You've successfully played the song 'Merrily We Roll Along'. This chord slash style is illustrated below. The 4/4 at the beginning means count and play four beats in every bar. If it was 3/4 at the beginning, what do you think it means? (The answer is that you would play and count three beats in the bar.) The bars are created by bar lines that look like this: '|'. It is usual to write four bars per line and then go to another line. In 'Merrily...' for example, the first bar is C for four beats, and the second bar is also C for four beats. The third bar is G7 for four beats, and the fourth bar is C for four beats. The next line is a repeat of the first line, so that the song has a total of eight bars altogether.

Merrily We Roll Along

4/4 C / / / | C / / / | G7 / / / | C / / / |
    C / / / | C / / / | G7 / / / | C / / / ‖
Merrily we roll along, roll along, roll along,
Merrily we roll along, over the deep blue sea.

This is going to take some practice. You may find that your fingertips become sore. The strings will buzz if you stop them in the wrong part of the fret or don't press hard enough. As you change chords while you strum, it's a challenge to jump your finger smoothly from the first string to the second string and back again. But don't get disheartened. Remember, everyone who has ever played the guitar – from Segovia to Pat Metheny to John Fahey to Eric Clapton – has had to go through this stage, and they found it just as awkward and just as frustrating.

The trick is to practise slowly and try to aim for good technique. Slightly arch your wrist, use your fingertips, and press firmly with your thumb in the middle of the back of the neck as you press down with your fingertip to stop the string. Try to eliminate all sounds of buzzing. Keep your other fingers out of the way.

Try this tune:

Go Tell Aunt Rhodie

4/4 C / / / | C / / / | G7 / / / | C / / / |
     C / / / | C / / / | G7 / / / | C / / / ||
Go tell Aunt Rhodie, go tell Aunt Rhodie,
Go tell Aunt Rhodie, the old grey goose is dead.

Chords D7 and G

Now let's try some more chords. The first chord is D7. This chord is going to use three fingers. Study the chord chart. Remember, each number represents a finger. (Third finger on second fret of first string; first finger on first fret of second string; second finger on second fret of third string.)

FIGURE 2-2(a):
D7

D7

FIGURE 2-2(b):
G

G

This chord is going to take some practice before it sounds clear. Work at it. A good exercise is to try to press hard and play the chord. Then relax your hand but keep the shape of the chord made by the fingers, raise them off the guitar strings, and then put the shape back on the strings – again, pressing hard. This may help build 'muscle memory', so that the fingers 'remember' where they should go to form this chord.

The next chord is the full open-string version of the chord of G. If you have trouble with this, just play the note on the first string and strum the first four open strings.

Twinkle, Twinkle Little Star

4/4 G / / / | C / G / | C / G / | D7 / G / |
    G / C /| G / D7 / | G / C / | G / D7 / |
    G / / / | C / G / | C / G / | D7 / G / ||

Twinkle, twinkle little star, how I wonder what you are
Up above the world so high, like a diamond in the sky,
Twinkle, twinkle little star, how I wonder what you are.

During this song, in the second and third bars and elsewhere, you'll play two beats of C and then two beats of G. This is a hard tune to play, so practise it a lot. The whole idea here is for you to get comfortable changing chords.

Amazing Grace

Note: This tune has a 'key signature' of 3/4. This means you strum three beats to the bar. Notice also that the second bar is blank. This means that you should repeat the previous bar. So bar two would be another three beats of G, as would be bar six. Bar eight will be three beats of D7, etc.

3/4 G / / | | C / / | G / / |
    G / / | | D7 / / | |
    G / / | | C / / | G / / |
    G / / | D7 / / | G / / | ||

Try these fuller versions of the chords C and G7, and then go back and practise the songs using the full versions.

FIGURE 2-3(a):
C

FIGURE 2-3(b):
G7

She'll Be Coming Round the Mountain

```
4/4 G / / / |      |      |        |
    G / / / |      | D / / / |        |
    G / / / |      | C / / / |        |
    G / / / | D / / / | G / / / |        ||
```

On the following pages are the full versions of some of the songs noted in this chapter. Use the tablature if necessary.

FIGURE 2-4:
Merrily

Merrily

FIGURE 2-5:
Aunt Rhodie

Aunt Rhodie

Twinkle, Twinkle Little Star

FIGURE 2-7:
Amazing Grace

Amazing Grace

FIGURE 2-8:
Coming Round
the Mountain

Coming Round the Mountain *

*Note: This is in a different key than in the text. See chord families in Lesson 3.

LESSON 3

Picking and more Open-String Chords

Right-Hand Picking

While you're still working on the chords you've already learned, let's look at some right-hand things you can study.

By now, you can see that holding and using a pick is a bit more complicated than just brushing the strings with your thumb. If you haven't done it already, play the songs in Lesson 2 using your thumb the first time through, and then the pick the next time through.

There are two distinct ways of hitting the string with a pick: a downstroke and an upstroke. To make a downstroke, use the tip of the pick and push down. The symbol is ⊓ .

Upstrokes are the reverse. The tip of the pick is used to pull up on the string. The symbol is V .

If you want to master using a pick, you need to become very comfortable mixing downstrokes and upstrokes. Otherwise, you will never develop any kind of speed and articulation in your playing.

FIGURE 3-1 includes some exercises to help develop right-hand picking. They use open strings and are written in both music notation and tablature. Things are a lot more complicated if you're left-handed, because you'll need a left-handed guitar. If you get one, then just do everything in a mirror image, substituting the left hand for the right hand and vice versa.

FIGURE 3-1:
Right-hand picking
exercises

One of the great things about this exercise is that you also learn to read music at the same time. (See, we told you it wouldn't be difficult.)

Minor Chords

Let's try a new chord. It's called a minor chord (written with a small m), and it has a sad or bluesy quality to it. Over the page are three minor chords: Am, Em and Dm.

FIGURE 3-2(a):
Am

Am

FIGURE 3-2(b):
Em

Em

FIGURE 3-2(c):
Dm

Dm

Drunken Sailor

4/4 Dm / / / | | C / / / | |
     Dm / / / | | C / / / | Dm / / / ‖

What shall we do with the drunken sailor?
What shall we do with the drunken sailor?
What shall we do with the drunken sailor?
Earl-eye in the morning

Wey, hey and up she rises,
Wey, hey and up she rises,
Wey, hey and up she rises,
Earl-eye in the morning

Swing Low, Sweet Chariot

4/4 (Swing) || D / / / | G / D / | D / / / | Em / A / |
　　　　　　　　D / / / | G / D / | D / A / | D / / /　 ||

Note: The first word of the song is in parentheses at the beginning, so you know where you are starting.

Auld Lang Syne

4/4 (Should) || G / / / | D / / / | G / / /　　| C / / / |
　　　　　　　　G / / / | D / / / | Em / Am D | G / / / ||
　　　　　　　　G / / / | D / / / | G / / /　　| C / / / |
　　　　　　　　G / / / | D / / / | Em / Am D| G / / / ||

Chord Families

Chords go together in families (or keys). For example, a G7 chord is part of the C family, and a D7 chord is part of the G family. Play those chords and they just seem to fit naturally together. A D7 chord, for example, does not lead to a C chord nearly as well as it leads to a G chord. Try it and see.

Chords break down into three basic types:

Major chords (like G or C), which sound happy.

Minor chords (like Am and Dm), which sound sad.

Dominant seventh chords (like G7 or D7), which sound slightly jazzy and seem to want to lead us to resolve to a major chord.

OK, now let's look at three more chords. These are part of the key (family) of A: E7, A and D.

FIGURE 3-3(a):
E7

E7

FIGURE 3-3(b):
A

A

FIGURE 3-3(c):
D

D

Yankee Doodle

4/4 D / / / | D / A / | D / / / | D / A / |
D / / / | G / / / | A / / / | D / / / ‖

Kumbaya

```
4/4 (Kumba-) || A / / / | / / D / | A / / / |           |
              A / / / | / / D / | E7 / / /\           |
              A / / / | / / D / | A / / / | / / D / |
              A / / / | / / E7 / | A / / / |        ||
```

When Johnny Comes Marching Home

```
3/4 (When)|| Am / / |        |        |        |
             Em / / |        |        |        |
             Am / / |        |        |        |
             C  / / |        |        |        |
             Am / / |        | Dm / / |        |
             Am / / |        | E7 / / |        |
             Am / / | E7 / / | Am / / | E7 / / |
             Am / / |        |        |        ||
```

In FIGURES 3-4(a), (b) and (c), are all the open-string chords you should learn. One of the things that makes learning chords easier is that families (keys) share the same chords, or variations on them. So once you know how to play a C chord or an E7 chord, it will be the same, regardless of the sequence you find it in.

Buy some song books, or look on the Internet for some song sheets you can download. Make sure they have the chords to the tunes printed on them so you can practise the songs.

Spend some time working on changing smoothly from one chord to another as you strum. Some of these chords involve using your first finger to stop more than one string. To do this, use the fatty part of your finger. Initially, you may want to lay your second finger on top of your first finger to help you make just enough contact with the strings on the fretboard so they don't buzz.

If you pay attention, you'll notice that some chords in the same key are missing. That's because they can't be played with open strings. You will soon learn how to play these chords.

FIGURE 3-4(a):
**Open-string
chords**

Key (family) of G

G C D7 Em

Key of A

A D E7 E7

(alternate fingering)

Key of C

C F G7 Am

FIGURE 3-4(b):
Open-string
chords

Key of D

D   G   A7   A7

(alternate fingering)

Bm

Key of E

E   A   B7

Key of F

FIGURE 3-4(c):
Open-string
chords

F   C7   Dm

Note in FIGURE 3-5(a) that each finger of the left hand should play a particular fret. The first finger plays the first fret, second finger plays the second fret, third finger plays the third fret, and the fourth or little finger plays the fourth fret.

Below is a left-hand fingering exercise. Notice that you should play this using each finger to a fret as we've discussed. (Normally, you would not play the B on the fourth fret third string, and also the open second string. But for the purposes of this exercise, go ahead and do it anyway.)

FIGURE 3-5(a):
Left-hand finger
exercises

FIGURE 3-5(b):

Each finger
to a fret

1st finger = 1st fret
2nd finger = 2nd fret, and so on
Practise alternate picking as well.

Overleaf is some sheet music for some more songs, the first of which you should recognize, which you can practise using what you've learned so far.

FIGURE 3-6:
Jingle Bells

Jingle Bells

FIGURE 3-7:
Simple Blues
in E

Simple Blues in E

FIGURE 3-8:
Simple Minor
Blues

Simple Minor Blues

LESSON 4

The Basics of Reading Music

Rhythm and Time

Having a good knowledge of 'where the beat is' and playing in time are paramount for a musician. As Duke Ellington once wrote, 'It don't mean a thing, if it ain't got that swing...'

Time breaks down into two elements: rhythm, or the 'feel' of a piece of music; and tempo, or the speed you play at. Music often has a suggested tempo marking on it which may look like this: ♩ = 120. The number 120 refers to the number of beats per minute (bpm) on a metronome. It denotes how fast (or slow) the piece should be played. The lower the number, the slower the piece of music. The higher the number, the faster the piece of music. In general, these are the accepted tempos (tempi, to be more precise), each of which has an Italian descriptive term.

Grave: very slow, slower than 40 bpm

Lento: slow, 40 to 60 bpm

Adagio: slow (at ease), 60 to 75 bpm

Andante: walking, 75 to 100 bpm

Moderato: moderate speed, 100 to 120 bpm

Allegro: fast (cheerful), 120 to 160 bpm

Vivace: lively, 150 to 170 bpm

Presto: very fast, 170 to 200 bpm

Prestissimo: as fast as possible, 200 or more bpm

Examples of rhythm include swing, folk, shuffle, merengue, pop, waltz, bossa nova, funk, heavy metal, country, bluegrass and so on.

Many musicians learn to play by playing along with CDs and records, or using a software program like Band-in-a-Box or a simple metronome that keeps the tempo rigidly. If you play along with a recording, you may have to retune your guitar slightly until it is in tune with the music. There are different ways of 'feeling the beat', which we won't go into here. It's enough that you get a grasp of the basic ideas of tempo and rhythm for now.

Written Music

As you've seen, we can write out music in tablature.

FIGURE 4-1:
Music in
tablature

Each line represents a string, and each number on a string represents a fret to use to play the note – a pretty good system for writing down tunes, you'd think. A version of this kind of music notation was used by Renaissance and medieval lute players.

The problem is, we can't easily use this kind of chart to show how long we should sound a note. One beat? Two beats? Three beats? How can you tell? While tablature is handy, it has its limitations.

So how do we solve that problem? We split the note up so that it lasts for different lengths of time – all of which are reflections of each other.

Semibreve: = 4 beats

Minim: = 2 beats

Crotchet: = 1 beat

Quaver: = half beat

Semiquaver: = quarter beat

The notes below a crochet have 'flags' attached to the stem. The number of flags on a stem will tell us the kind of note we're playing – one flag for a quaver, two for a semiquaver.

Time Signatures

As we've seen already, we write 4/4 at the front of a piece (or 3/4, and so on). The top number (4 or 3) tells us how many beats in the bar to count. The bottom number tells us the kind of note we are counting (in this case, a crotchet). So if 4/4 means four crotchets to each bar, and 3/4 means three crotchets per bar, then 2/2 – also known as cut time – would be what? You've got it: two minims to the bar. What would 6/8 be? Right: six quavers to the bar. And so on.

The notes in the bar have to add up to whatever the time signature says. For example, 3/4 would mean the notes must add up to three. Then a bar line | is drawn, and we start the next group of three. If the notes had to add up to four, then we would make sure there was a bar line every time the notes added up to four.

For example, these notes all add up to four:

One semibreve

Two minims

Four crotchets

Eight quavers

16 semiquavers

These notes add up to three:

One minim and a crotchet

Three crotchets

Six quavers

12 semiquavers

What if you don't want a note to be played? Or you want one note to last longer than usual? Each of the notes has a corresponding rest note, which indicates that you should not play for that brief period. So you could also make up beats by inserting a minim and a crotchet rest, or a minim rest and a crotchet, or two crotchets and a crotchet rest, and so on. See FIGURE 4-2 overleaf.

FIGURE 4-2:
Rests

If we write a dot immediately after a note, it will increase that note's duration by half as much again. For example, a dotted semibreve would be four beats plus two, totalling six. A dotted minim would be two beats plus one, totalling three. A dotted crotchet would be one beat plus half a beat. (In this case, the next note would start on the 'offbeat'.)

Another way to make a note last longer – and keep everything neatly within the bar lines – is to tie two notes together. In FIGURE 4-3, for example, you play the first note, keep your finger down and continue to count for the length of the second note that is tied to the first with a curved bar connecting the two notes.

FIGURE 4-3:
Tied notes

Basic Elements

There are only seven notes in the musical alphabet, and then they repeat themselves: C-D-E-F-G-A-B (then C again, which is considered an octave, or eight notes higher than the first C you played). You can start the sequence on any note you like, but it still repeats after seven notes. (For example, A-B-C-D-E-F-G-[A]; F-G-A-B-C-D-E-[F], etc.)

There are two basic elements to reading and writing music: the name of the note in the musical alphabet you want a musician to play; and how long that note should last. Over the years, these two elements became combined into one elegant system called musical notation. A five-line 'stave' developed, and the note's position and appearance on the stave told musicians what note to play and how long to hold the note before playing the next note.

The modern stave is split into two halves, each of which is called a clef, and each of which has a particular sign at the beginning to tell us which stave we are using. These clefs are called the treble clef and the bass clef. When piano players read music, they play the treble clef with their right hand and the bass clef with their left hand.

Notes that appear below or above the clefs appear on what are called ledger lines – individual lines for each note – but we won't worry too much about them for the moment.

Look at FIGURE 4-4. Between the treble clef and the bass clef is one note on a ledger line. That note is called middle C because it is the note C and it falls between the two clefs. It is usually played on the guitar as the note on string 5, third fret. (Actually, middle C should be an octave higher, but we won't bother with that now.)

FIGURE 4-4:
Middle C

Because the notes on the lines and the spaces make up the musical alphabet in sequence, the note on the space after middle C is D. The note on the next line is E, on the next space F, and so on.

The great thing about the guitar is that you only have to learn the notes on the treble clef. If we look at all the notes on the lines, beginning with middle C, we see that they are:

FIGURE 4-5

The notes on the spaces above middle C are:

FIGURE 4-6

Combining the lines and spaces, we get:

FIGURE 4-7

All pretty easy and simple, really, particularly if you play the piano. However, those of you who are quick off the mark may have found a little problem when it comes to playing the guitar. You may have noticed when you practise tuning up that you can play the same note (as it appears on the treble clef) in different places on the guitar. E, on the top space, for example, can be played on string 2, fifth fret, or on string 1, open. For the moment, we won't bother too much with this problem, as we're going to confine ourselves to reading music in the first position – that is, around the first fret. (Incidentally, the solution to the problem was developed by Segovia. Above the notes, you indicate the string you should use.)

Let's recap what we know, using notation.

FIGURE 4-8

Finding the Notes on the Guitar

Now we just need to find out where these notes are on the guitar. This section includes some exercises on the open strings that have fingerings to help you learn the musical alphabet.

FIGURE 4-9

(Bass Strings)

FIGURE 4-10

(Treble Strings)

Now go back to some of the songs in the last two lessons and try reading the music notation.

Dynamic Markings

When we talk about dynamics, we basically mean how loudly or how softly you play the note or the chord. Again, the dynamic markings in music have Italian names. Here they are with their symbols:

pp: pianissimo, very quietly

p: piano, quiet

mp: mezzo piano, moderately quiet

mf: mezzo forte, moderately loud

f: forte, loud

ff: fortissimo, very loud

Staccato means 'short and detached'. When you play staccato, you keep the rhythm of the piece, but you play the notes for a shorter duration than you normally would. Staccato notes are often marked with dots underneath them.

The opposite of staccato is legato, which means 'smooth'. Here you slur the notes together, maybe playing one note and hammering down on the next note using left-hand fingering alone.

FIGURE 4-11:
Exercise in
counting notes

Key Signatures

As we've seen, notes can be on lines (E-G-B-D-F) or spaces (D-F-A-C-E-G) on the stave. We can also raise or lower these notes one fret or half step using sharp (♯) to raise and flat (♭) to lower. Instead of placing lots of sharps or flats into some tunes, we can instead put these sharps or flats at the beginning of a piece of music, which then tells us all the notes that have a sharp or flat sign in front of them. These notes should be played that way unless a natural sign (♮) tells you otherwise. If an additional sharp or flat is needed, the sign is placed before the note to which it refers; it is then used for that note for that specific bar only.

What's more, depending on how many sharps or flats there are at the beginning of a piece of music, we can tell which key the music is written in.

One flat = key of F
Two flats = key of B♭
Three flats = key of E♭
Four flats = key of A♭
Five flats = key of D♭
Six flats = key of G♭

Six flats (or altered notes) are just about as many notes as you need to remember. After this we get into what are 'enharmonic' notes, or notes that have the same name, such as 'C flat', which is really B natural. As a result, we usually start to think about sharp keys at this point.

No sharps or flats = key of C
One sharp = key of G
Two sharps = key of D
Three sharps = key of A
Four sharps = key of E
Five sharps = key of B
Six sharps = key of F♯

FIGURE 4-12:
Key signatures

When you're comfortable with all this, try the next couple of tunes.

FIGURE 4-13:
Polly Wolly
Doodle

Polly Wolly Doodle

Drunken Sailor

FIGURE 4-14:
Drunken Sailor

We Wish You a Merry Christmas

LESSON 5

More Right-Hand Techniques

Basic Rhythm Guitar

This lesson will help you explore some of the possibilities of playing the guitar by concentrating on what the right hand does. Right-hand technique is often the major element in defining the difference in style between genres such as folk, country and rock and roll.

Let's start with some strumming or rhythm exercises using a pick.

Most of the time you've just been playing downstrokes (unless you've been adventurous and tried to include some upstrokes as well, as shown on page 159). To this point, you've determined how many beats in the bar to count based on the time signature (4/4, 3/4, etc.). Now let's explore the possibilities of accents and different rhythms.

You should use a metronome for these exercises. Pick any chord – an E chord, for instance – and try these exercises. Try to keep time so well with the metronome that the sound of the tick disappears. Most important, try to make your time and chord changes as fluid as possible and as close to the metronome ticks as possible. If you mess up the change, don't worry. Good time is more important here than good articulation. That will come with practice. If it helps, change between an E and an Am chord every time there is an accent to play.

Now let's work on some rhythm guitar and accents. Try this exercise to develop your rhythm guitar playing:

FIGURE 5-1(a)

An X indicates a rhythm beat, not a note to be played. It's how drummers write music for themselves. Remember, the symbol ⊓ means a downstroke. The symbol V means an upstroke.

FIGURE 5-1(b):
Rhythm exercises

(— = accent this beat)

(With all these exercises, vary the upstrokes and the downstrokes.)

count: 1 + 2 + 3 + 4 +

Triplet feel

A shuffle beat, which has
a triplet feel, can be best counted:
TWIN-KLE TWIN-KLE
LIT-TLE STAR.

count: 1 + a 2 + 3 + a 4 +

Basic Alternating Bass Picking

Play an E chord. Play string 6 open with your pick, and then strum the rest of the chord using a downstroke, like this:

FIGURE 5-2

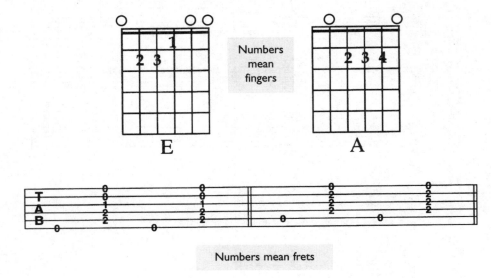

This 'boom-chick' kind of sound can be turned into alternating bass. Playing the bass note on string 6 for the E chord and then the bass note on string 5 for the A chord starts to develop a pattern.

Eventually, you can really develop long bass note runs this way, suggesting a bass player accompanying the guitar (or, if you prefer, the idea that you are playing left and right hands on a piano). However, to begin with, just keep things very simple, with one bass note per chord. The coordination needed to play like this and sing along is really hard, so don't get upset if it all falls apart the first few times you try this.

FIGURE 5-3:
Wabash
Cannonball

Wabash Cannonball

Listen   to the   jingle   the   rumble   and   the

roar   as   she   glides   along   the   woodlands   through

hills   and   by   the   shore.   Hear   the   mighty   rush   of   the   engine   hear   the

lonesome   hoboes   call   you're   traveling   through

jungle   on   the   Wabash   Cannon - ball.

Basic Finger-picking

There's a difference between classical right-hand position and folk and blues-style right-hand positions, but the essence of the right-hand styles is the same.

FIGURE 5-4:
Right-hand
position

In its basic form, the right-hand thumb plays the three bass strings, the first finger plays the third string, the second finger plays the second string, and the third finger plays the first string. The stroke comes from the finger joints, not the knuckle.

FIGURE 5-5(a)

right-hand fingers

(open strings)

FIGURE 5-5(b)

For a good classical technique, it's best to grow your nails slightly, so that you get a nice percussive attack, and slightly arch your wrist so that the fingers are vertical to the strings.

The difference between the hand position in folk/blues right-hand picking and classical guitar playing is one of degree. Note that while the folk/blues position seems more relaxed, it can also cause some muscle strain if you're not careful.

Go back and practise the early pick exercises using your fingers instead of the plectrum to play the treble strings.

Folk Picking

Now that you have some basic ideas about how the right hand can work, let's explore some right-hand finger patterns used in various forms of music. We'll start with folk music. As you learn new songs, experiment with these different right-hand patterns.

FIGURE 5-6(a)

FIGURE 5-6(b)

Pattern 5 Carter style

(Play the notes with stems down with your thumb.)

Pattern 6 Travis style

Step 1: Set up a bass pattern.

Step 2: Add a treble string, keeping the bass steady.

Step 3: Add a second treble string, keeping the bass steady.

Step 4 (last step): Pinch the first string and fifth string together.

Note that you use your thumb to play the bass notes. Also, pinch together a bass note and a treble string so that you can pick out the melody of a tune while giving the impression you're keeping a steady bass line going. This takes lots of practice, but can sound really cool!

Basic Blues

The following illustration shows some basic blues rhythms to start you off.

FIGURE 5-7

The next one shows a 12-bar shuffle blues rhythm in tab form.

FIGURE 5-8:
12-bar blues
in A

Country Picking

An advanced form of right-hand picking combines holding a pick and using the fingers at the same time. It's pretty hard to do, but it's popular with country players and some jazz musicians who play solo guitar. Often it entails the technique of using the little finger of the right hand.

FIGURE 5-9

LESSON 6

Beyond the Basics
and Movable Chord
Shapes

The Whole Enchilada...

So far you've learned that the musical alphabet consists of seven letters: A-B-C-D-E-F-G. Actually, there are five other notes in the musical alphabet, which are variations on the seven letters you already know.

Think back to the piano keyboard image we showed you in the section on tuning a guitar.

Did you notice that there were a number of white notes and black notes that weren't named? Let's fill in those spaces.

FIGURE 6-1:
Black notes

As you can see, some notes have a ♯ (sharp) sign in front of them, and some have a ♭ (flat) sign in front of them. These notes are called accidental notes. Look again, and you'll notice that the same note can be called either a sharp note or a flat note. How is that possible?

Semitones

In Western music (as opposed to music from the Middle East and the Far East), musical notes move in semitones or half-steps. These semitones correspond to the keys on a piano. The black keys represent the sharp/flat keys, and the white keys represent the musical alphabet as you currently know it. On a keyboard, you can see that in two different places there are two white notes together. Otherwise, the keys alternate white notes with black notes.

Starting from E on the open string 6, there is a semitone between E and F. (This is the first pair of white notes that go together. We'll discuss this in the lesson on harmony.)

Between F and G there is a black note, which we can call either F♯ (F sharp), which is a semitone up from F, or G♭ (G flat), which is a semitone down from G. (F♯ and G♭ are said to be enharmonic notes – that is, they're actually the same.) Between G and A there is another black note, called G♯ or A♭ for the same reason; similarly, between A and B is a note called either A♯ or B♭.

Between B and C there is a semitone. (This is the second pair of white notes that go together.) Between C and D is C♯ or D♭; and between D and E is D♯ or E♭. Then we're back to E again.

Chromatic Scale

All 12 notes together make up the musical alphabet and form what is called a chromatic scale. This is all you need to know to play and read music. See, we said it was easy.

As we've mentioned before, music is about what notes to play (melody), and how long you should play them (rhythm). The only other element you need to learn is harmony (which is what happens when you play two or more notes together at the same time). Again, we'll discuss this in the lesson on harmony.

Here is the complete chromatic scale, moving in semitones from the note E:

E, F, F♯/G♭, G, G♯/A♭, A, A♯/B♭, B, C, C♯/D♭, D, D♯/E♭, (E).

This is how it looks written out in standard musical notation:

FIGURE 6-2:
Chromatic scale

Note:
♭ = sharp
♯ = flat
♮ = natural (see below)

In musical notation the sharp (♯) and flat (♭) signs come in front of the note. A natural sign (♮) in front of a note means that you play that note without making it sharp or flat – as it is played naturally.

How the Guitar Fits in

So how does the guitar fit into all this? You may recall that we said each fret of the guitar is a semitone away from the next. So the guitar fretboard naturally forms a chromatic scale. Very useful.

If you play E, string 6, open, and then the note on every fret on the E string up to the 12th fret, you will have played a chromatic scale starting on E. Try it.

If you play A, string 5, open, and then the note on every fret up to the 12th fret, you will have played a chromatic scale starting on A, and so on.

The next figure shows all the notes on all the strings.

FIGURE 6-3

This is a really important concept, because now you can do lots of things on the guitar fretboard, not just confine yourself to open-string chords. The most important thing you can do is move the same chord shape up and down the neck!

Movable Chords

The idea that you can move one shape up and down the neck and play lots of chords at the same time is pretty amazing. These chords are called movable chords.

You already know there are different types of chords. You've learned about major chords, minor chords and seventh chords (also called dominant seventh chords). You've probably wondered how these different types of chords get their names. Why E, or C, or G7 or Am? We'll go into this in more detail in the harmony chapter. For now, all you need to know is that a chord has a name (or root) note. This note is usually found somewhere on one of the three bass strings.

For example, the name (root) note of E is on string 6, open.

FIGURE 6-4

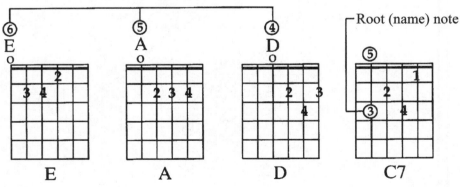

2 = second finger
3 = third finger
4 = little finger

The name note or root note of A is found on string 5, open, and the name/root note of D is found – where? Right, on string 4, open.

Look at the last chord in the previous figure. It's a new chord, called C7. It gets its name from the note on the third fret on string 5. When you play it, don't play string 6 or string 1; just play the inner four strings.

Using the same fingering, move that chord shape up two frets. Your third finger, on string 5, should now be at the fifth fret, and your first finger should be on string 2 at the third fret. (The other two fingers should be in the same pattern as the diagram, obviously. We're moving shapes here, right?)

Remember, this chord gets its name from the note on string 5. Look at the chromatic scale, look at your fingers on the fretboard (you are trying to play this chord, right?), and try to figure out what the name of this chord should now be. The question is: what's the name of the note on string 5 at the fifth fret?

Moving a C7 chord shape from the first position (your first finger is playing a note on the first fret) to the third position (first finger is now playing a note on the third fret) means that the new chord is called D7.

'Wait a minute', we hear you cry, 'don't you play D7 a different way? In Lesson 2, you distinctly said a D7 chord should be played this way.'

FIGURE 6-5

D7

You're absolutely right. In fact, you can play the same chord in different ways all over the guitar neck. (We'll talk about this in more detail later on.) Here's the thing: play the D7 chord as you originally learned it. Now play it using the new shape you've just learned. It's the same chord, but somehow it sounds subtly different. So you now have a choice of ways to play D7, depending on how the chord sounds. Besides, with a little practice, you'll find that it's much easier to change from chord to chord using movable shapes.

Barre Chords

Barre (pronounced 'bar') chords are a special kind of movable chord. You create them by using your first finger to stop all the strings across a fret, and then you play a movable shape over it. Don't panic; it's pretty easy, although it takes a little practice.

Put your first finger across all six strings at the first fret. If you have trouble getting all the notes to sound clearly, put your second finger on top of your first to help press it down until the notes ring clearly. Relax. Flex your fingers. Now try it again. Move your first finger to the second fret, play the strings, then relax your hand. Repeat this at the third fret, and then the fourth – and so on – trying to get a clear sound from each note on the strings as you do it. Use that first finger to stop all the frets in turn as far up the neck as you can go, playing all the strings at a fret, relaxing your hand and then trying again, all the time making sure that the notes on each string sound clear, and don't buzz or sound muffled. Like everything else with the guitar, it gets easy with a little practice.

Now look at the notes on string 6. If the root note, or name note, for the E major chord is string 6, open, then theoretically, if you move the E shape up one fret, you move the root note up one fret as well.

Use your first finger to barre the strings on the first fret. Use the suggested fingering to play an E shape chord at the first position/fret while you barre the first fret with your first finger. This is not easy, but persevere. Try to get all the notes on all the strings to sound clear when you play them. Relax your hand.

The note on the first fret of string 6 is F. That means that an E shape chord, which in the open-string position is called E, in the first position (that is, at the first fret) is called F. Move it up to the third fret, and now it is called G.

Quick test – try to find and play these chords:

G♭, F7, C♯7, A♭, E♭7, and F♯. (Hint: you'll find the root notes of all these chords on either string 6 or string 5.)

Having trouble with this exercise? Take a break, have a cup of coffee, and then re-read this chapter until you're comfortable with the concept we're talking about and you can find these chords. It's really not that hard. Honest.

Go back through some of the earlier lessons and try playing the songs using the movable chord shapes you've learned.

Movable Shapes

FIGURE 6-6 shows movable chord types gathered together based on the location of the root note. Some of these chords have fingerings that are not that easy because they involve using more than one finger to barre more than one fret – A, for instance, or Dm7 – but with a little practice, you'll get it.

FIGURE 6-6:
E-shape:
major, maj

E-shape:
dominant 7,
7, dom7

(alternate fingering)

E-shape:
minor, m

minor

E-shape:
minor7, m7

m7   m7

(alternate fingering)

A-shape:
maj (double
barred chord)

maj   maj

A-shape:
dom7

dom7

A-shape:
minor, m

A-shape:
minor7, m7

D-shape:
maj

D-shape:
dom7

D-shape:
minor, m

m

D-shape:
minor 7, m7

m7

C-shape:
maj (half barre)

maj

dom7

Movable Chords with Muted Notes

Up until now we've haven't made much of a fuss about which strings you strum when you finger a chord. It's been enough that you get the strings to sound out clearly without buzzing or making some other noise while you fret the notes and play.

At the beginning of this lesson, we asked you to play a C7 chord. We also said, '*Don't* play string 6 and string 1, just the middle four strings.' What we did, in a way, is mute or deaden the sound of string 6 and string 1 so that they wouldn't sound when you played the chord. That's because while the open note E is part of a C7 chord, if you move that chord shape up the neck, the note E clashes with the other C7 shape chords that you play that *don't* contain the note E in them. We'll explain more about why this is important in the lesson on harmony.

A muted chord is one in which you must deaden (or mute) one or two strings while you play the chord. You mute the strings so that you get the correct key tones out of the chord shape every time you play it, wherever you play it.

FIGURE 6-7

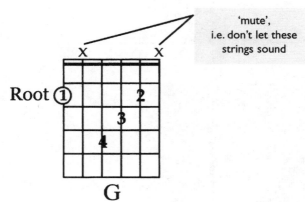

This figure shows a movable G chord with two strings (that is, notes) crossed out with an *x*: string 5 and string 1. That means you shouldn't let these strings sound when you play the chord. A pretty tall order, right? Even knowing about barre chords, haven't we just spent a whole book saying you should make the notes ring out clearly? Well, the answer is yes – and no. As you get better at playing the guitar, you'll find that some things that are good to do when you're beginning are not so good to do when you become more advanced.

To mute a string, you need to shape your hand in such a way that these two strings are dampened or deadened when you strum a downstroke. To sound the note, we've told you to use the tip of your finger on your left hand. To dampen or mute a note, use the fatty or flat part of either the side of your finger or just under your fingertip, depending on the kind of chord you're trying to play. Now play each of the remaining notes of the chord until they sound clear. Play the notes individually (called an arpeggio) to make sure you have them right.

Here are the five basic seventh chords in muted forms:

FIGURE 6-8:
maj7

maj7

dom7

dom7

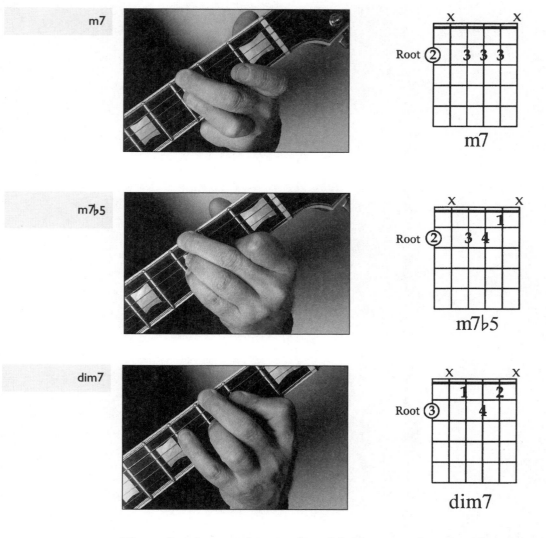

m7

m7♭5

dim7

These chords sound very colourful. If you can learn to play them well, you'll get a great feeling of achievement.

We don't have the room here to really explore this whole concept of movable chords and muted chords, but there are lots of books available on the subject, a few of which are listed in the Appendix. Here we've tried to give you an idea of how this works, and show you how you can go forwards if it's something that appeals to you.

LESSON 7
Playing
in Position

Position Playing

Well, you've come along quite a way! By the time you've mastered the concept of movable chords and the material in this chapter – playing in position – you'll be able to think of yourself as an intermediate player.

Up to now we've pretty much covered the basic things you can do using the open strings or, as it is more accurately called, in the open position. The simplest way to think of position playing is to think about where your first finger lies on the guitar neck. We talked about left-hand fingering in Lesson 3. You tried an exercise (FIGURE 3-5 (a)) in which each finger of the left hand had a fret it covered. The first finger played notes on the first fret, the second finger played notes on the second fret, the third finger played notes on the third fret, and the fourth finger played notes on the fourth fret.

Strictly speaking, to play a chromatic scale we should only play three notes on string 3 because the fourth fret (B) is the same note as string 2, open (B), and there's no need to repeat. So try the chromatic scale again using the proper fingering.

FIGURE 7-1:
Chromatic scale
fingering

Using the open strings, we are playing in the open position. If we start this exercise on F (first fret string 6) and play it as shown in the following figure, then we are playing in the first position, because that is where the first finger is lying on the guitar fretboard.

FIGURE 7-2:
First position
chromatic scale

(Note: Slide your fourth finger up one fret to play the notes on the fifth fret.)

Let's explore this idea a bit more. The idea of position playing changes how we look at the guitar fretboard. Up to now, we've been thinking about moving around the guitar fingerboard as going up and down the neck vertically – say from the first fret to the second, third, fourth and so on – moving chord shapes from one fret to another in order to get different chords. The problem here is that you can end up jumping all over the neck trying to play two chords or notes one after the other. There ought to be a more efficient way of doing things – and there is.

FIGURE 7-3

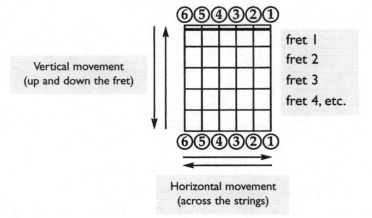

Vertical movement
(up and down the fret)

fret 1
fret 2
fret 3
fret 4, etc.

Horizontal movement
(across the strings)

In position playing, we're starting to think about playing within the same number of frets but moving horizontally *across* the fingerboard – that is, from string 6 to string 1 – so your fingers aren't jumping all over the neck looking for notes and chords. This is another important concept.

Playing a Scale

Let's move to the second position. That means the first finger will play all the notes on the second fret, and the other fingers will play the next four frets (second finger plays third fret, third finger plays fourth fret, fourth finger plays fifth fret).

Let's play a C major scale in position. In the next figure, look at the fingering. Even though the first note C is played on the third fret with the second finger, we're still in the second position because of where the first finger is. The Roman numeral II denotes the space above the second fret.

FIGURE 7-4:
C major scale in
second position

One of the great things about playing in position is that it becomes much easier to read music. It may seem that the easiest place to read music on the guitar is in the open position, but really, only the first four notes on string 6 have to be played in this position. Everything else can be played somewhere else.

Let's get really adventurous and play in the seventh position.
(Remember, that means the first finger covers notes on the seventh fret.)
Look at the following figure and play the scale.

FIGURE 7-5

Again, the Roman numeral VII means the seventh fret.

FIGURE 7-6(a)

We can also extend the scale and play it again (making two octaves).
Look at the fingering.

FIGURE 7-6(b)

Movable Patterns

Wait a minute, didn't we just play that? Indeed we did. It's the C major
scale, this time starting on string 6 at the eighth fret. But hang on there –
the finger pattern was the same as in the second position.

That's the trick about position playing. Because you aren't using open strings, you can really concentrate on a pattern of fingering and then move that pattern around the fingerboard, producing predictable results. If you learn, for example, that the fingering pattern for a major scale is 2–4, 1–2–4, 1–3–4, then you can play any major scale you like on string 6 and string 5. All you need to know is the name of the starting note.

But Wait, There's More...

If we play in the second position we can easily play the notes E, F, G♭, G and A♭ on string 6, but we can only play up to the note A on string 1, fifth fret, comfortably. That means if you have to read a piece of music that doesn't have a note higher than this range, the best place to play the music would be in the second position.

FIGURE 7-7

	E	E
Fret 1	F	F
Fret 2	G♭	G♭
Fret 3	G	G
Fret 4	A♭	A♭
Fret 5	A	A

The range of notes in the second position.

Look at 'Daisy Bell' (opposite). You can see that the highest note you have to play is A on the second fret, string 3, while the lowest note is A on string 5, open. So we can play the piece in the second position.

FIGURE 7-8:
Daisy Bell

Daisy Bell

Now let's try playing in the seventh position. It's really easy. The only notes you haven't learned yet are the notes on string 1 starting on the fifth fret – A, B♭, B, C, D♭, D.

FIGURE 7-9

Here's the written range.

Now try the next exercise.

FIGURE 7-10:
Seventh position
exercise

Shifting Position

Of course, music doesn't have to be played in just one position – and it really shouldn't be. Very often we start in one position and then shift to another position, using what is called a position shift. Basically, all this means is that you move your first finger to a new place on the neck and the other fingers just naturally follow along.

Key Centres

You learned earlier that when we move the position of a chord, it becomes a different chord. For example, if you move an E shape chord to the fifth fret (fifth position), you're really playing an A chord. You can take that idea a little further here, by thinking of the fourth and fifth position as a good place to play chords, improvise solos and so forth in the key of A. You'll need to experiment with this idea, but, trust us, it works. (Move one fret higher and suddenly you are playing in the key of B♭.)

Similarly, you can play in the key of G at the second and third positions, or the key of C at the seventh and eighth positions. It also means that unusual keys like B♭, F♯, D♭ or B are really exactly the same as G or C or D, they're just at a different fret position. With a minimum of effort, you can suddenly play in any key, as long as you know the best position in which to play the key. Just remember, the first finger is the guide to moving the hand around the fingerboard, either vertically or horizontally.

LESSON 8

Basic
Harmony

What is Harmony?

Harmony is such a vast subject that people can study it for the whole of their musical career without ever reaching the end. It's fascinating, and if you let it, it can take you on a journey from the rural Delta blues of Mississippi to the songs of the Beatles; from the rock and string compositions of Frank Zappa to the jazz composition and arrangements of Duke Ellington, Fletcher Henderson, Charlie Parker, John Coltrane and George Russell; from the jigs and reels of Scotland and Ireland to the vast continent of classical music composition by such composers as John Dowland, Beethoven, Bach, Debussy, Stravinsky, Vaughan Williams, John Cage and many, many more.

Yet at the root of all these vast and differing ways to make music are the same basic ideas: melody, rhythm and harmony. We've already looked at melody, which is when notes follow each other to make up a tune; and rhythm, which is basically about how long each of the notes should be played for, and how often. Now, we'll look at the third element, harmony, which is what happens when you play two or more notes together at the same time.

Yes, it's true that anything sounds good (at least to the composer) if you believe in it. However, most people expect music to sound a certain way, and as a result there are 'rules' about how, when and why certain notes should go together. Even if you're a punk headbanger, a John Cage fan or into some other form of experimental music, to really push the envelope it's best that you have some understanding of the rules that you're about to break.

And frankly, there are still questions we can't answer. We can tell you, for example, *what* a major chord or a minor chord is, but we can't tell you *why* it's called a major chord or a major scale. Some things it's best you just accept – at least for a while.

What we are going to look at applies equally to all the keys – to any key, in fact. But to make it easier to understand, we're going to look at everything in the key of C. The key of C does not naturally have any sharps or flats (accidentals), so the variations and so forth can be more easily seen.

Here is the scale of C major. Notice that the notes fall alternately on lines and spaces. For example, C is on a ledger line, D is on a space, E is on a line, F is on a space, and so on.

FIGURE 8-1:
C major scale

C   D   E   F   G   A   B   C

Intervals

Let's start with the concept of the distance between two notes, which is called an interval. You'll remember that we said the frets of a guitar are a semitone or half-tone apart (same thing, different name). Well, a semitone is the smallest interval, or distance, between two notes – at least in Western music. This is the distance from C to C♯. (C♯ is one semitone up from C, remember, and D♭ is enharmonically the same note, a semitone down from D.)

A whole tone (usually just called a tone), which is two semitones, would be from C to D. This would be the equivalent of jumping to a note two frets away on the guitar.

It's very helpful not only to know this information intellectually, but also to see how you can apply it to your instrument. Look at the fingerboard.

The distance from C, third fret, string 5 to C♯, fourth fret, string 5 is a semitone.

The distance from C, third fret, string 5 to D, fifth fret, string 5 is a whole tone.

Intervals by Semitone

From C to D♭ is a minor second – that is, one semitone.

From C to D is a second – that is, two semitones.

From C to E♭ is a minor third – three semitones.

From C to E is a major third – four semitones.

From C to F is a fourth – five semitones.

From C to G♭ is a diminished or flattened fifth – six semitones. If we say the interval is from C to F♯ (enharmonically the same note as G♭, remember), this can be called an augmented fourth. Flattening – or diminishing – a note means dropping it down a semitone or fret. Augmenting a note means sharpening or raising it a semitone or fret.

From C to G is a fifth – seven semitones.

From C to G♯ is an augmented fifth (also called a raised fifth) – eight semitones. In the same way as before, C to A♭ (enharmonically the same note) is a minor sixth.

From C to A is a major sixth – nine semitones.

From C to A♯ is an augmented sixth – ten semitones. In the same way, from C to B♭ is a minor seventh – ten semitones.

From C to B is a major seventh – 11 semitones.

From C to C is an octave – 12 semitones.

FIGURE 8-2:
Intervals written
as notation

Scales

Both major scales and minor scales are created by putting together a series of tones and semitones. Of course, depending on whether the scale is major or minor, these tones and semitones are arranged in a different sequence.

Major Scale

There are lots of good books on harmony, and it's not necessary now to know all the theory that goes into creating scales. If you're interested, you should take a look in the Appendix for some books you can start with.

If we look at the major scale again, we can see it is built this way:

C to D – tone
D to E – tone
E to F – semitone
F to G – tone
G to A – tone
A to B – tone
B to C – semitone

So the pattern for any major scale is tone, tone, semitone, tone, tone, tone, semitone.

Minor Scale

Each major scale has a corresponding minor scale (called the relative minor), built on the sixth note of the major scale. There are three different types of minor scales that we can study: the harmonic minor, the melodic minor and the natural minor. Each scale is built slightly differently from the other.

The natural minor scale is the easiest to start with because it's composed of all the notes of the related major scale (in this case, C), starting on the sixth note of the scale.

FIGURE 8-3

C major scale

A natural minor scale
(starts on sixth of C scale)

A harmonic minor scale consists of tone, semitone, tone, tone, semitone, minor third, semitone.

FIGURE 8-4

A harmonic minor scale

C harmonic minor scale

In the key of A minor, it would be called A harmonic minor:

A to B – tone

B to C – semitone

C to D – tone

D to E – tone

E to F – semitone

F to G♯ – minor third

G♯ to A – semitone

In the key of C it would be C harmonic minor, and would be built this way: C-D-E♭-F-G-A♭-B-C.

A melodic minor scale is more complex because it is often played in classical harmony as ascending in one form and descending in another. However, for our purposes we'll learn it the same way going up and down.

The melodic minor is built of tone, semitone, tone, tone, tone, tone, semitone. In the key of A melodic minor it would be A-B-C-D-E-F♯-G♯-A. In the key of C melodic minor it would be C-D-E♭-F-G-A-B-C.

FIGURE 8-5

A melodic minor scale

C melodic minor scale

Chord Structures

The combination of three or more notes is a chord. Three-note chords are called *triads*. Four-note chords are called *seventh chords*.

Triads

There are four types of triads: major, minor, augmented and diminished, which are built by piling major thirds and minor thirds on top of each other in different combinations. You can 'spell out' the four triad chords this way:

Cmaj	C-E-G	major third minor third
Cm	C-E♭-G	minor third major third
Caug	C-E-G♯	major third major third
Cdim	C-E♭-G♭	minor third minor third

Most chord structures are a variation on these four triads.

The following figure gives you an example of how these triads can be played on the guitar.

FIGURE 8-6:
Triads

maj triad   min triad   dim triad   aug triad

On the guitar, these simple chords are not usually spelled this way. For example, you can mix up the order of the notes, and instead of playing C-E-G, you can play G-C-E. You can also double notes. An E maj triad is spelled E-G♯-B, for example, but it is usually played E-B-E-G♯-B-E.

It's not really important now to know these structures inside out. Instead, learn the chord forms on the chord diagrams. Try to figure out where other triads can be played on the guitar and write them down for yourself.

Seventh Chords

Four-note chords are called seventh chords. They generally have much more colour and sound more interesting than triads. Furthermore, they are the basis of all our standard repertoire of tunes. To make a seventh chord, add either a major third or a minor third to one of the four triad forms. Doing this, we get five basic seventh chords, with other chords being variations on these five.

In the key of C, the five are:

Cmaj7	C-E-G-B	
C7	C-E-G-B♭	(also called a dominant 7)
Cm7	C-E♭-G-B♭	
Cm7♭5	C-E♭-G♭-B♭	(also written C≠7 or C half diminished)
Cdim7	C-E♭-G♭-A	(the last note is usually called B double flat, but we'll call it A, which enharmonically it is)

As you've seen, we can make chords up by piling thirds on top of each other. Another way to look at chords is to build them from the tones of a scale (major or minor – it doesn't matter).

Here's a C major scale again:	C	D	E	F	G	A	B	C
Let's put numbers underneath:	1	2	3	4	5	6	7	8
Let's use Roman numerals:	I	II	III	IV	V	VI	VII	VIII

A chord can be built by choosing every other note in the scale and then altering it if necessary:

Cmaj7	1-3-5-7
C7	1-3-5-♭7
Cm7	1-♭3-5-♭7
Cm7♭5	1-♭3-♭5-♭7
Cdim7	1-♭3-♭5-♭♭7

Again, while on the piano keyboard it is relatively easy to play these chords as we've spelled them out here, on the guitar that isn't the case. A Cmaj7 chord, for example, is often played on the guitar spelled C-G-B-E, or C-B-E-G.

If you spend some time working on understanding how chords are built, you'll soon be able to build your own. For example, if you know how to play a Cmaj7 chord, and suddenly you are confronted with Cmaj7♯5, you just need to play a Cmaj7 shape, work out which note is the fifth of the chord, and raise it up a fret (semitone) to make the ♯5 part of this chord. (The chord, of course, would be spelled 1-3-♯5-7—that is, in the key of C: C-E-G♯-B.)

We said earlier that there are five basic seventh chords. That's true, but there are seven more chords that are variations on these five. Here are the full dozen:

Cmaj7	1-3-5-7
C7	1-3-5-$\flat$7
Cm7	1-$\flat$3-5-$\flat$7
Cm7$\flat$5	1-$\flat$3-$\flat$5-$\flat$7
Cdim7	1-$\flat$3-$\flat$5-$\flat\flat$7(6)
Cmaj7$\sharp$5	1-3-$\sharp$5-7
Cmaj7$\flat$5	1-3-$\flat$5-7
C7$\sharp$5	1-3-$\sharp$5-$\flat$7
C7$\flat$5	1-3-$\flat$5-$\flat$7
Cm maj7	1-$\flat$3-5-7 (C minor major 7)
C6	1-3-5-6
Cm6	1-$\flat$3-5-6

Think about this – a m6 chord and a m7$\flat$5 chord are the same thing, although they will have different root notes: Cm6 = Am7$\flat$5.

Arpeggios

An arpeggio is simply a 'broken' chord. In other words, if you play individually the notes that make up a chord – say Cmaj7, (C-E-G-B) – you are playing a Cmaj7 arpeggio. To play these arpeggios properly, you should learn them in two octaves. For example, C-E-G-B-C-E-G-B-C.

Single-note arpeggio practice (meaning playing one note of a chord at a time) is a wonderful way of getting these sounds in your head. It's also a terrific basis for learning how to improvise over a chord sequence in a tune or song.

Diatonic Chords

If you go through a major scale, building chords on every note of the scale by using every other note, you get what we call diatonic chords – all the chords that naturally occur in the key.

In the key of C, these are Cmaj7, Dm7, Em7, Fmaj7, G7, Am7, Bm7♭5, Cmaj7.

If you go through a harmonic minor scale, you get this sequence:

Cm maj7	Dm7♭5	E♭ maj7♯5	Fm7	G7	A♭ maj7	Bdim7	Cm maj7
I	II	III	IV	V	VI	VII	VIII

Standard Progressions

What we mean by *standard* here is 'generally accepted' or 'normal'. There are standard tunes such as 'Over the Rainbow', 'Moon River' and even 'Happy Birthday to You' that are created using certain chord progressions, which means that a chord naturally progresses to another chord after it's played. (A G7 chord, for example, naturally progresses to a Cmaj7, partly because G is the fifth note in the scale and key of C.)

If you go back and look at the seventh chords in the key of C, each has a Roman numeral under it. There's a reason for this. Instead of saying Cmaj7-Fmaj7-G7, for example, we could just say I IV V. Then we could look at the notes of *any* major scale, and play the I IV and V chords built on the first, fourth and fifth notes of the scale. (They would be a maj7, maj7, dom7 sequence of chords.)

Cycle of Fourths and Fifths

If you go back to Lesson 4 and look at the section on key signatures, you may notice something now. If you follow the key signatures carefully, you'll see that from C to F is a fourth, and from F to B♭ is a fourth, and so on through the flat keys. Similarly, C to G is a fifth, G to D is a fifth, D to A is a fifth, and so on through the sharp keys. In fact, a fourth in one direction is a fifth in the other.

FIGURE 8-7:
Cycle of fourths
and fifths

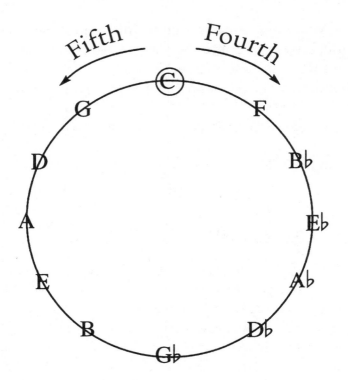

You've seen that we can use Roman numerals instead of chords. Following the flat keys (the notes that are a fourth away from each other), we get a series of V I chords. That is, C7 resolves to Fmaj7; F7 resolves to B♭maj7; B♭7 resolves to E♭maj7; E♭7 resolves to A♭maj7; A♭7 resolves to D♭maj7; D♭7 resolves to G♭maj7; G♭7 resolves to Bmaj7; B7 resolves to Emaj7; E7 resolves to Amaj7; A7 resolves to Dmaj7; D7 resolves to Gmaj7; and G7 resolves to C.

Practise this sequence using muted and movable chords.

The Blues

To finish, let's look at a fun and usable progression: the blues. A blues sequence is really just a I IV V sequence. So a blues in B♭, say, would be B♭ maj7, E♭ maj7, F7.

Here's a basic 12-bar blues in C (using triads).

```
4/4  C / / / | F / / / | C / / / |          |
     F / / / |         | C / / / |          |
     G / / / |         | C / / / |     ||
```

However, this is a bit bland and could do with some colour. Let's use dominant seven chords:

```
4/4  C7 / / / | F7 / / / | C7 / / / |          |
     F7 / / / |          | C7 / / / |          |
     G7 / / / |          | C7 / / / |     ||
```

A slightly more complicated sequence is I VI II V. This sequence is the basis of most standard tune chord progressions. Using the diatonic chords you learned about earlier, in the key of C this would be Cmaj7, Am7, Dm7, G7. If you analyze songs by working out their key signatures, you'll discover that this I IV II V sequence is used in a lot of them.

One of the things you may well discover is that the root notes in the VI II V I sequence are all a fourth apart. (In the key of C: A to D to G to C.) Next time you play a song, look for this pattern and this sequence. The more you practise using this cycle of fourths, the easier playing standard song progressions becomes.

Try this jazzy blues sequence:

```
4/4  C7 / / /  | F7 / F♯dim7 / | C7 / / / | Gm7 / C7 / |
     F7 / / /  | F♯dim7 / / /  | C7 / / / | A7♯5 / / / |
     Dm7 / / / | G7 / / /      | C7 / / / | (G7♯5 / / /) ||
```

When you practise chords and scales, try to do this in the cycle of fourths sequence. First, play a C major scale, then an F major scale, then a B♭ major scale, and so on.

APPENDIX A

Glossary

A

accent: A dynamic effect that places an emphasis on a note or chord.

accidentals: Symbols in written music to raise (♯ – sharpen) or lower (♭ – flatten) notes by semitones. A double flat (♭♭) lowers the pitch by a tone. A natural (♮) cancels the accidental alteration.

acoustic guitar: A hollow-bodied guitar that does not require electronic amplification to be heard fully.

action: The strings' playability along the neck. Action is affected by the strings' distance from the neck, the neck straightness and the string gauge.

altered chord: A chord or scale in which one or more of the notes is changed to a note not normally associated with that scale.

archtop: A guitar, often an acoustic, with a curved top (soundboard) and F-holes similar to those of a violin.

arpeggio: Literally, 'like a harp' – i.e., playing the notes of a chord one after the other rather than together. Also known as a broken chord.

artificial harmonics: Harmonics produced by fingering a note on the frets and lightly touching the string a fourth higher.

atonal: Not part of the tonal system of major and minor keys; in no key at all.

augmented (see also *diminished*)**:** Intervals increased by a semitone are known as augmented intervals. The augmented chord is a major chord with the fifth raised a semitone.

B

barre: A special kind of movable chord created by stopping all the strings across a fret with your first finger and playing a movable shape over it.

bebop, hard bop: A style of jazz that emerged in the 1940s, using fast melodic lines over adventurous extended harmonies. The terms bop and bebop are interchangeable, and hard bop usually refers to the 1950s blues-influenced variant.

binding: Thin strips of wood or plastic that seal the edges of the body of a guitar.

blues: An African-American style of music that uses a scale including flattened thirds, fifths and sevenths, known as the 'blue notes' in a scale. A blues style has a predominantly 12-bar form, although the likes of Charley Patton and John Lee Hooker often break the rules.

body: The main part of the guitar, to which the bridge and neck are attached. On acoustic guitars and some electrics, the body serves as a resonating chamber.

boogie-woogie: A style of blues and jazz with a repetitive rhythmic bass figure derived from early jazz piano-playing.

bossa nova: A Brazilian rhythmic style of jazz and popular music widespread in the United States and Europe in the 1960s.

bottleneck guitar: A technique using a metal or glass tube, rather than the fingers of the left hand, to play notes and chords, and to slide from one fret to another.

braces: Interior wooden strips that strengthen a hollow-bodied guitar. Brace size and configuration partly determine a guitar's tone.

break: In jazz, a short solo passage without accompaniment that usually occurs at the end of a phrase.

bridge: The structure that holds the saddle (or saddles), over which strings pass on the guitar body. Most bridges can be adjusted to raise or lower string height, changing the guitar's action and intonation.

C

capo: A spring-loaded, adjustable clamp that becomes in effect a 'movable nut'. It fits over the neck and covers all the strings at a given fret, raising the pitch of the strings and allowing a singer or flamenco player to play in a different key and still use open-string chords and fingering.

chamber music: Music for small groups of players (usually no more than nine). The term chamber jazz is sometimes used for the more formal style of small combo such as the Modern Jazz Quartet.

changes: The sequence of chords used as a basis for improvisation in jazz.

choking: Damping the strings of the guitar with the fingers or the palm of the hand to give short staccato chords.

chord: Any combination of three notes played together, usually based on the triad formed by the first, third and fifth notes of the scale. For example, the chord of C major consists of C (the root of the chord), E and G. Chords can be in root position – that is, with the root as the bass note – or various inversions using other notes in the chord as the bass.

chord substitutions: In jazz, alternatives to the conventionally used chords in a sequence.

chorus: On an electric guitar, a chorus pedal simulates the effect of more than one instrument playing the same note.

chromatic: Chromatic notes are those that fall outside the notes of the key a piece of music is in. The chromatic scale is a 12-note scale moving in semitones.

classical: The term classical is used to describe art music, to distinguish it from folk, jazz, rock, pop and so forth, although the boundaries are becoming blurred.

comping: Jazz jargon for accompanying.

compression: On an electric guitar, this boosts the volume of quieter notes and reduces that of louder ones, evening out the sound of fast passages.

counterpoint, contrapuntal: The playing of two or more tunes at the same time within the same harmonic framework. The added tunes are sometimes called countermelodies.

country (and Western): A predominantly white, rural popular music originally from the Southern and Western USA.

cutaway: An indented area of the body that allows the guitarist's fretting hand to access notes higher up the neck.

D

delay (echo): On an electric guitar, delay mimics the echo effect by playing a delayed copy of the original sound.

detuning: Intentionally putting one or more of the strings out of standard tuning for a specific effect.

diatonic: Using the notes of the major scale.

diminished: Intervals decreased in size by a semitone are known as diminished intervals. The diminished chord is based on intervals of a minor third, and the so-called diminished scale consists of alternating tones and semitones.

distortion: Change of tone quality, with a harsh sound, achieved by overdriving an amplifier, or with the use of a distortion pedal, fuzz box or overdriver.

double-stopping: Forming a chord by stopping two or more strings with the left hand on the frets.

double or (multi) tracking: Recording technique enabling a player to superimpose a number of parts onto a particular piece.

dreadnought: A large-bodied, steel-strung acoustic guitar.

drone strings: Strings not intended to be played with the fingers, but tuned to vibrate in sympathy with the main instrument's strings.

E

effects: Numerous special effects are possible on a modern electric guitar, including *chorus, compression, delay, distortion, enhancer, expander, flanger, fuzz, harmonizer, Leslie, octave divider, overdrive, panning, preamp, reverb, tremolo, vibrato, volume pedal* and *wah-wah* (see separate listings for each).

enhancer: On an electric guitar, a device to improve sound definition.

expander: The opposite of *compressor*, increasing the range of volume on an electric guitar.

F-holes: Violin-style F-shaped soundholes, usually found in pairs.

feedback: The loud whine produced by a microphone or pickup receiving and amplifying its own signal from a loudspeaker.

fill: In jazz and rock, a short melodic figure played by an accompanying instrument between phrases.

finger-picking: Right-hand technique in which the strings are plucked by individual fingers.

Flamenco: A Spanish style of playing, singing, and dancing. Forms of flamenco include *alegrias*, *buierias*, *fandangos*, *farrucas*, *ganadinas*, *malaguena*, *seguidillas*, *siguiryas*, *soleas* and *tarantas*, and the guitar often interjects *falsetas* (melodic improvised interludes) into these forms. Techniques in flamenco guitar-playing include *alzapua* (up-and-down strokes with the thumbnail), *apagado* (left-hand damping), *golpe* (tapping on the body of the guitar), *picado* (fingerstyle) and *rasqueado* (strumming by unfurling the fingers across the strings).

flanger: On an electric guitar, a chorus-type effect, using a delayed signal with a slight pitch variation.

flat-top: A guitar whose soundboard, or top, is flat.

fretboard: The wooden strip, usually of hardwood, attached on top of the neck, into which the frets are set. Also called the fingerboard.

frets: Metal wires set into the fretboard at precise distances, allowing the strings to sound the correct pitches along the neck.

folk: The music of rural cultures, usually passed down orally. The word 'folk' is also used to describe composed music in the style of true folk music, particularly after the folk revival of the 1950s.

free jazz: A jazz style of the 1960s, which is freely improvised without reference to a specific tune or harmonic sequence.

fusion: Originally, a blend of jazz and rock, but also any form of crossover from one style to another.

fuzz: On an electric guitar, a form of distortion, operated by a fuzz pedal.

gig bag: A portable padded bag, made of canvas, nylon or leather, that you can use as an alternative to a hard case. It zips shut and offers about the same protection as a piece of soft leather luggage.

glissando: A slide from one note to another.

grace notes: Short notes played just before the main note of a tune as an ornament.

groove: A repeated rhythmic pattern in jazz and rock.

guitar synthesizer: Guitars with built-in synthesizers for dramatically altering the sound, or equipped with MIDI to control external synthesizers, drum machines and so on.

habañera: A Cuban dance, or its rhythm.

hammer-on: Notes played by hammering the string with the fingers of the left hand, rather than plucking with the right hand.

harmonics: Notes with an ethereal tone higher than the pitch of the string, produced by lightly touching a string at certain points.

harmonizer: On an electric guitar, a chorus-type effect adding a sound in harmony with the original signal.

head: In jazz, the statement of the tune before and after the improvised solos.

headstock: The structure at the end of the neck that holds the tuning machines.

I

interval: The distance between two notes. For example, C to G is a fifth (that is, five notes of the scale); C to E is a third (three notes); and C to C is an octave (eight notes).

inversion: see *chords*.

J

jazz: African-American in origin, characterized by the use of improvisation, blue notes and syncopated rhythms.

L

Latin: Music of Latin-American origin, including dance rhythms such as the *habafiera*, samba, rumba, bossa nova and so on.

legato: Smoothly, not staccato.

Leslie: The Leslie cabinet, originally for use with electronic organs, contains a rotating speaker, giving a swirling effect to music played on an electric guitar.

licks: In jazz and rock, short phrases that are inserted into a solo or used as fills.

M

machine head: See *tuning peg*.

microtone: Interval of less than a semitone.

MIDI: Musical Instrument Digital Interface. This allows musical instruments such as electric guitars and synthesizers to communicate with sequencers, effects boxes, computers and so on.

minimalism: A movement in music from the 1960s using static harmonies, repeated patterns and a minimum of material.

modes: Scales using the notes of the diatonic scale, other than the major and minor scales. The modes, such as Dorian, Phrygian and Aeolian, originated in medieval music, but were adopted by jazz players in the 1950s.

modulate: To move from one key to another.

N

neck: The long structure that runs from the body to the headstock, and onto which the fretboard is attached. Necks have a longitudinal curve that can be adjusted by means of the truss rod. The width, shape and curvature of the neck largely determine the action and playability of a guitar.

nut: The notched fitting – usually of bone, ivory, ebony, metal or plastic – that guides the strings from the fretboard to the tuning pegs.

O

octave divider: On an electric guitar, an early form of *harmonizer*, adding a sound an octave above or below the original signal.

open tuning: Tuning the strings of the guitar to a specific chord, rather than the conventional E-A-D-G-B-E, often for slide work. There are also other non-conventional tunings, such as D-A-D-G-A-D.

overdrive: On an electric guitar, a form of distortion.

overdubs: Parts added to a recording after the original take.

P

panning: On an electric guitar, moving the source of the sound within the stereo field.

partial chords: Chords not using all the strings of the guitar.

passing chords: Chords used in passing from one harmony to another, not part of the main harmonic sequence.

pedal note: A repeated bass note that supports a sequence of changing harmonies.

pentatonic: A scale of five, rather than the more usual seven, notes.

phasing: On an electric guitar, playing two identical sounds slightly out of phase with one another.

pick or plectrum: Object used for striking the guitar strings, usually made from plastic.

pickguard: A protective plate on the body of the guitar that protects the top from being scratched by a pick or fingers.

pickup: The device on electric guitars that picks up and transmits the sound of the strings to the amplifier.

pickup switch: Allows pickups to be turned on individually or in various combinations.

potentiometer (pot): A variable resistor used for an electric guitar's volume and tone controls. Amplifiers also have pots.

preamp: With an electric guitar, the preamplifier can be used as a form of tone control, or to boost the signal.

pull-off: A note played by pulling the string with the fingers of the left hand.

R

raga: A scale used in Indian music. There are hundreds of different ragas, many using microtones.

ragtime: An African-American style of music, a precursor of jazz.

reverb: On an electric guitar, this mimics the echo effect, either by a built-in spring reverb or a digital electronic emulation.

rhythm and blues: African-American pop music originating in the late 1940s, the precursor to rock and roll.

riff: In jazz and rock, a short, repeated melodic phrase.

rock, rock and roll: Rock evolved in the 1950s from rhythm and blues, and in its 1960s form became known simply as *rock*.

rubato: Not strictly in tempo – played freely and expressively.

rumba (rhumba): An Afro-Cuban dance.

S

saddle: The fitting that guides the strings over the bridge. Most electric guitars have individual saddles for each string. These can be adjusted to change a string's length and thus its intonation.

scales: A series of ascending or descending notes in a specific key, the basis for compositions in the tonal system.

segue: Moving without a break to the next movement, section or whole piece.

semitone: A half tone. The smallest interval in the diatonic scale – for example, the distance between E and F, or B and C.

serial, 12-tone: Avant-garde compositional method using the 12 notes of the chromatic scale in series, without reference to traditional harmony or tonality.

slide: A style of guitar-playing using bottleneck or lap slide, where notes and chords slide from one to another.

solid body: A guitar whose body is made from a solid piece of wood or is a solid lamination. Most electrics have solid bodies, but some are semi-hollow.

soundboard: The resonating top of an acoustic guitar.

soundhole: A hole (or holes) in the top of an acoustic guitar through which sound is emitted.

staccato: Detached. Staccato notes or chords are short and clipped, not moving smoothly to the next.

straight eights: In jazz, playing *straight eights* means playing exactly on the beat, whereas *swing* indicates that the rhythm should be interpreted more freely. (See also *swing*.)

string-bending: Using the fingers of the left hand to pull a string to one side, 'bending' the pitch of the note.

strings: The cords that are plucked to cause vibrations that produce a guitar's sound. Most guitar strings are solid wire or thin wire wrapped around a solid core; classical guitars have nylon and metal-wound nylon strings. A string's thickness (gauge) depends on its position on the guitar and the relative thickness of the entire set.

swap fours: In jazz, when soloists alternate improvisations with one another every four bars.

swing: A style of jazz of the 1940s, mainly for big bands. Also an instruction to play rhythms freely. (See also *straight eights*.)

syncopation: Shifting the accent of a melody off the main beat of the bar – a characteristic of jazz and much rock and pop music.

T

tailpiece: The device that holds the strings' ball ends on archtop and some electric and flat-top guitars.

tempo: The underlying speed of a piece of music.

timbre: The tone quality of a sound.

tonal, tonality: Relating to the system of major and minor keys.

tone (whole tone): An interval of two semitones – for example, the distance between C and D, or F and G.

tremolo: On an electric guitar, small and rapid variation in the volume of a note. This effect is often confused with *vibrato*. The tremolo arm or bar is used to bend the pitch of notes on electric guitars.

trill: Rapid alternation between one note and the note above.

truss rod: A metal rod that runs through the length of the neck, increasing its strength and allowing adjustment of the longitudinal curve. Some guitars have two truss rods.

truss rod adjusting nut: The part of the truss rod system that can be tightened or loosened to alter rod tension.

tuning pegs: Devices set into the headstock that anchor strings and allow them to be tuned. Each tuning machine consists of a post, a geared mechanism and a tuning key. Also called machine heads.

turnaround: In jazz, the harmony under the last phrase of a tune, taking the music back to the beginning for its repeat.

unison: On exactly the same note. In jazz, the tune of the head is often played by several instruments in unison.

vamps, vamping: Repeated accompanying figure in jazz and popular music before the melody begins.

vibrato: On an electric guitar, small and rapid variation in the pitch of a note.

voicing: The spacing of the notes in a chord.

volume pedal: Means of altering the volume of sound for an electric guitar, useful in creating a fade-in effect or as a swell pedal.

wah-wah: With an electric guitar, the wah-wah pedal controls the relative bass and treble response of a sound. Fully down, it has a high treble tone; fully up it emphasizes the bass. The characteristic 'wah-wah' sound is achieved by rocking the pedal back and forth.

whole-tone scale: A six-note augmented scale formed entirely of intervals of a whole tone, such as C-D-E-F♯-G♯-A♯.

Method Books
and Other Music Books

Most of these books are available on Amazon.co.uk and should be readily available in a good-sized music shop:

Mickey Baker, *Mickey Baker's Jazz Guitar*

William Bay, Mike Christiansen, *Mastering the Guitar:*
A Comprehensive Method for Today's Guitarist (Mel Bay Publications).
This is a seven-book series.

Gene Bertonicini, *Approaching the Guitar*

Terry Burrows, *The Total Guitar Tutor*

Tom and Mary Anne Evans, *Guitars: From the Renaissance to Rock*

John Fahey, *American Primitive Guitar*

Mick Goodrich (Pat Metheny, contributor), *The Advancing Guitarist*

Ted Greene, *Modern Chord Progressions*

William G. Leavitt, *Modern Method for the Guitar: Vols 1, 2, 3*

John Mehegan, *Jazz Rhythm and the Improvised Line Jazz Improvisation*

Frederick M. Noad, *Solo Guitar*

Mark Phillips and John Chappell, *Guitar for Dummies*

Aaron Shearer, *Classical Guitar Technique*

Nicolas Slonimsky, *Thesaurus of Scales and Musical Patterns*

Tommy Tedesco, *For Guitar Players Only*

APPENDIX C

Guitar Tricks

Hammer-On

This is used a lot in rock, blues and folk playing. Fret a note with your first finger, say D at the fifth fret, string 5. Now, while the note is still ringing, 'hammer' down your finger on E at the seventh fret, string 5, and keep it there.

Pull-Off

This is really a hammer-on in reverse. You need to have both fingers on the fret. Play the note E, as before, then pull off your finger so the D will sound clearly.

Trills

If you rapidly combine both techniques above, you get a trick often used in rock and roll that may sound familiar, called a trill.

String Bends

A lot of rock guitarists and blues guitarists use a string bend. If you pull or push the string across the fretboard, once you've fretted the note, you can actually bend it almost to the note on the next fret. It's the same sort of technique as using a mechanical tremolo arm. It generally works best if you use thin-gauge strings.

Double String Bends

In this rock and blues trick, you need to have both fingers in place ahead of time. Here, you play the D on the seventh fret of string 3, bending it until you've reached the pitch of E, and – while still sounding the bent note – play E on an adjacent string (fifth fret, string 2), letting the two notes ring together.

Another trick is to play the D and E together (major second), fingering them as above, and then bend the D into an E, letting the two Es sound together.

Vibrato

This just means deliberately invoking a 'wow-wow' kind of effect. All you do is rock your finger back and forth on the note as you fret it. The more exaggerated the movement of your hand, the broader will be the vibrato.

Slide

This is simple. Slide your finger from one fret to another while the note is still ringing.

APPENDIX D

Websites
for the Guitar

Jack Wilkins's Website
www.jackwilkins.com

Curt Sheller – Guitarists' Links
www.curtsheller.com

One of the best general sites about the guitar for beginners
http://guitar.about.com/musicperform/guitar

Guitar at About – Online Guitar Lessons and Jazz Transcriptions
http://guitar.about.com

International Online Jazz Guitar Newsletter
www.musicweb-uk.com

Guitar Resources on the World Wide Web
www.cmeabaysection.org/guitres.html

All JAZZ GUITAR – The Online Community for the Jazz Guitar Enthusiast
www.mindsync.com/kerin/donprice

Online Guitar Chord Dictionary
www.lib.virginia.edu/dmmc/Music/GuitarChords

***Rolling Stone* magazine's Website**
www.rollingstone.com

Educational Site
http://VisionMusic.com

AMG All Music Guide
www.allmusic.com

Progression – Playing – Guitar
www.progression.co.uk/playing

GuitarSite.com – Home of *Guitar News Weekly* & the 2000 Guitars Database
www.guitarsite.com

APPENDIX E

More Scales
and Chord Shapes

FIGURE APP1:
Major scale
fingerings
(two octaves)

Work out the others for yourself. Practise playing through the cycle of fourths.

FIGURE APP2:
Minor scale
fingerings

Natural   Harmonic   Melodic

Work these out in two octaves.

FIGURE APP3(a):
Pentatonic scales

Pentatonic, or five-note, scales (used widely in blues and rock)
Work these into two octaves and practise through the cycle of fourths.

FIGURE APP3(b):
Augmented scale

Augmented scale (AKA whole tone scale)
As the name suggests, it moves in whole tones only.

FIGURE APP3(c):
Diminished scales

There are two different types of scales, as shown above.
Work out in two octaves and play through the keys.

FIGURE APP3(d):
Basic seventh chord shapes

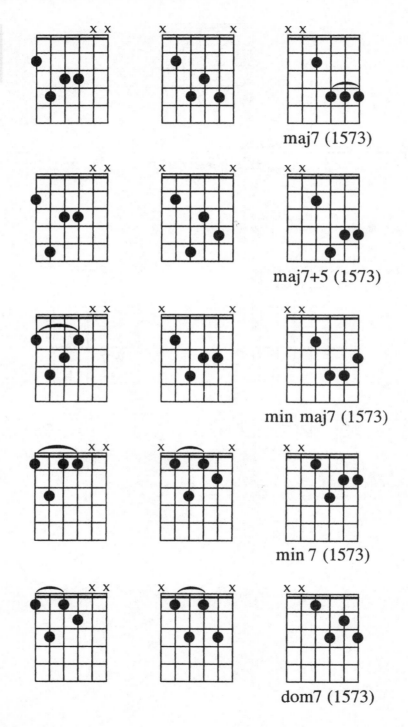

maj7 (1573)

maj7+5 (1573)

min maj7 (1573)

min 7 (1573)

dom7 (1573)

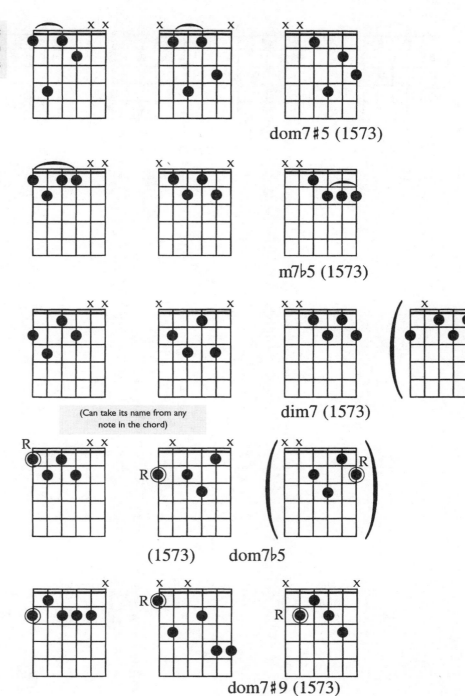

FIGURE APP3(e):
Basic seventh chord shapes

dom7♯5 (1573)

m7♭5 (1573)

(Can take its name from any note in the chord)

dim7 (1573)

(1573)   dom7♭5

dom7♯9 (1573)

FIGURE APP3(f):
Basic seventh
chord shapes

Chord shapes 3

dom7♭9

Index